VENICES

PAUL MORAND

VENICES

Translated from the French by
Euan Cameron

with an Afterword by
Olivier Berggruen

PUSHKIN PRESS
LONDON

First published with the title *Venises* © Éditions Gallimard 1971

Translation copyright © Euan Cameron 2002

This edition first published in 2002 by
Pushkin Press
123 Biddulph Mansions
Elgin Avenue
London W9 1HU

British Library Cataloguing in Publication Data:
A catalogue record for this book is available
from the British Library

ISBN 1 901285 41 3

Frontispiece: Harlingue´Viollet
Photographs: Roger-Viollet, Paris
Cecil Beaton photograph courtesy of Sotheby's, London

Set in 10 on 12 Baskerville
and printed in Britain
by Sherlock Printing, Bolney, West Sussex
on Legend Laid paper

VENICES

LIST OF ILLUSTRATIONS

I

THE PALACE
OF THE
ANCIENTS

ALL OF OUR LIVES are letters posted anonymously;
my own bears three postmarks: Paris, London and
Venice; fate, often unwittingly, though certainly not
thoughtlessly, has decreed that I should have settled in
these places.

Within her restricted space, Venice, situated as she is in
the middle of nowhere, between the foetal waters and
those of the Styx, encapsulates my journey on earth.

I sense a disillusion with the entire planet, apart from
Venice, apart from the Basilica of St Mark's, whose blis-
tered, declivitous paving looks like prayer mats set side by
side; the fact that I have known St Mark's all my life
thanks to a watercolour that used to hang in my bedroom
as a child: it was a large wash-drawing painted by my
father in about 1880—bistre and sepia, and sketched in
Chinese ink—a piece of late romanticism, in which the
red of the altar lamps pierces through the domes of golden
dusk, and in which a turbanned throne is illuminated in
the Western light. I also possess a little oil painting that
belonged to my father, a view of the Salute on a grey day,
which is of unusual delicacy and which has always been
with me.

"One must see Venice after it has been raining", Whistler
used to say: it is after experiencing life that I have
returned here to think about myself. Like the tarred spars
that stake out her lagoon, Venice has delineated my life;
yet she is merely one among other points of perspective;

11

Venice has not been my entire life, but she constitutes a few fragments of it that are otherwise disconnected; her tide marks fade away; mine do not.

I remain impervious to the absurdity of writing about Venice, at a time when even the primacy of London and Paris is no more than a memory, at a time when the nerve centres of the world are remote spots such as Djakarta, Saigon, Katanga and Quemoy, where Europe can no longer make her authority felt, and where only Asia matters. Situated at the gates of that continent, Venice had understood this, and had penetrated as far as China; it is to Marco Polo that St Mark's should be dedicated, not the other way round.

In Venice, my insignificant being had its first lesson on this planet, as I emerged from classrooms in which nothing had been learnt. School for me was nothing but endless boredom, exacerbated by justified reprimands; if there was still ink on my fingers, nothing remained in my head, and the weight of those books! Lugging the Quicherat dictionary from the Champs-Élysées to the Lycée Monceau, along a route which those who have not climbed the rue de Courcelles each morning reckon to be flat crushed my narrow city-dweller's shoulders. The tarmac was hard beneath my feet; I was already thinking of Venice, and I was determined to celebrate that aquatic city, in which every street was the Seine.

The classic authors did not appeal to me; they had written for the courtiers of Versailles, or for teachers; nothing about our great writers intrigued, gripped or shocked me; what connection was there between the Atreids with their golden masks, which Schliemann had just excavated, and the bewigged Atreids of the seventeenth century? Starting one's life with *Bérénice*! Appreciating *Bérénice* at the age of thirteen! First I would have had to have fallen in love with someone who loved Racine; who could explain Racine to me, explain this heart of a woman grafted on to a man's body? No one provided me with a key to words, every other one of which meant something different to what it does today; I went from one misinterpretation to another: *la gloire*? reasons of State? A king who cried? Nuances are not children's toys. How could a woman be both gentle and violent? On the other hand, I became thoroughly involved in Shakespeare, with his crimes and his ghosts, as I listened to Marcel Schwob and my father, who were translating *Hamlet* together for Sarah Bernhardt—an infinitely more appetising translation than Gide's—searching among the English for some old French word, rather as one might discover a primitive painting beneath a later work. Shakespeare, that towering puppet-master, in whose plays everything, instead of being sliced into four parts, was reconciled and overcome.

I have never learnt grammar;[1] it's nothing to be proud of, but it seems to me that if I were to learn it today, I should no longer be able to write; my eye and my ear were my only teachers, the eye especially. Good writing is the opposite of writing well. "There are not enough words to express what I think…": that's because instead of thinking, you were searching for words; it's up to the words to search for you, up to them to find you. You should be able to say of any one of your sentences: "it's the spitting image of its father." A writer should have his own wavelength.

The philosophy classes of my youth were merely the annexe of some miserable psychiatric hospital; geography merely provided me with a catalogue of gulfs and islands, an inventory of mountain tops and rivers, a repertory of peaks as bare as the mountains of the Moon; apparently no human being had ever lived there; as for History, its artificial discontinuities, its famous "turning-points" and the arbitrary divisions of its reigns precluded me from appreciating anything apart from battles, or treaties that were destined to pave the way for further battles.

As I look back with hindsight over the long years, what astonishes me are the curious omissions and the possibly tendentious silences of the early instruction I was given. I was taught nothing about pre-history, Byzantium, China and the Far East, the United States or Russia, about religions or music; I left my *lycée* knowing neither the names nor the voyages of the famous explorers, being totally ignorant about economic geography, the history of Art, biochemistry and astronomy; not having read Montaigne, Hugo or Baudelaire, or the poets of Louis XIII's reign, not Dante, Shakespeare or the German Romantics ... Colonna d'Istria, my philosophy teacher, who was fascinated by malfunctions of the will, devoted six out of nine months to this subject, before dashing off logic, morals, metaphysics and the history of philosophy in a few hours; at Sciences Po,[2] Émile Bourgeois made us spend two years dozing over the King's dusty secret. Who was responsible for these Ubuesque gaps which life had been unable to fill, for this inadequate instruction, wedged in between primary school certificate and the final degree, for this pit-ridden educational landscape through which I stumbled: the syllabus, the teachers, or my lapses of application and intelligence?

I hungered for nothing.

It may seem scarcely credible that I should speak of being uncivilised and narrow-minded. On top of my instinctive pessimism, education came and added the books that I was surrounded with, those from the family library: the Renan of the post-1870 years, Schopenhauer, Zola, Maupassant, Huysmans, the grinding of their teeth, their grim laughter.

I was an only son, a solitary child, and the first adages my father taught me were the following, so typical of Mérimée: *Remember to mistrust yourself* [3] or *Your friends may one day be your enemies*; he was a father whose philosophy could be summed up as follows: "The Creator failed with this world; why should he succeed with the next one? Everything has been bungled, and always will be. It is only Art that does not lie."

This may explain my anxious, withdrawn temperament, for during my first fifteen years, although not shy, I kept myself very much to myself and I was unaffectionate and unsociable; my childhood was not the precocious state of wonderment at the outside world that it was for the majority of writers, from Gide to Alain-Fournier, from Proust to Montherlant. I remained on my guard. As a result, I was late developing.

I have always felt that childhood was an inferior form of existence. I was sensible, accustomed to a quiet life, and respectful of the God-given virtue of thrift. I had reached my student years never having loved, understood, seen or experienced anything. Are the great discoveries of life reserved for old age?

Venice is the backdrop to the finale of the grand opera that is an artist's life: Titian died there after his *Deposition*, Tintoretto after *San Marziale*, Verrocchio after the *Colleone*. The one consolation is that one lives to a great age there: Giovanni Bellini was eighty-six years old, Longhi eighty-two, and Guardi eighty-one.

Is it fate, or is the fault to do with me: I always arrive when the lights are being switched off; no sooner had it started than it was over; I have witnessed the end of the nineteenth century; the end of a secondary education system that had lasted forever (1902); of one-year military service (1906); of the disappearance of the gold exchange (1914); I have seen several Republics die as well as one État; and two empires expire; beneath my gaze I have witnessed a whole herd of staunch or foolish famous men disappear, as well as a few moments of glory. I am drawn towards that which is ending; it is not merely the fact that I have attained a great age, it is also a curse, the burden of which I can feel.

I am bereft of Europe.

I have inherited my father's physique, a robust one what is more; as well as almost everything else. My energy stems from further back. Did I love him, or was it what I saw of myself in him? Even today, I cannot manage to make the distinction. As a child, I had the sense that my existence depended on him, and that if he were to disappear, the house would collapse.

When famous men extol the virtues of their mothers, they describe them to us as exceptional people, as victorious athletes in the dedication stakes, breaking all records of selflessness, as monsters of magnanimity or phenomena of goodness. My mother was so united to my father, so serene a soul, so self-contained, and so perfectly Christian that she would have hated to be held up as an example. She was a Jansenist, but one possessed of such charm! Her patience, tolerance and her good humour were very much in evidence, and it was these very qualities that made for such an equable home life. Her gentle virtues, her natural reserve and her moral qualities were a challenge to no one, and were not put forward as an example, as was the case with Proust's mother, or Gide's; her cultural background was a humble one, neither Jewish nor Protestant, but one appropriate to the religion, country and class to which she had been born, in the heart of the Marais. She wore very flowing clothes, known at the time as *kasha*, their muffled beige colours, like her blond hair, relieved only by her black gloves or the veil of black chiffon that fell from her hat and wrapped itself around her neck.

I was a non-believer, more in imitation of my father and in order to become a man than to upset my adorable mother; the men in my family would set off to meet their wives after Mass, but they ventured no further than the entrance to the church. The State was hostile to religion,

silent, not anti-clerical, but extremely radical. I was
unable to understand the catechism, a dialogue in which
I was interrupted without obtaining the answers to the
questions I wanted to ask. It was not the unknown that dis-
oriented me in matters of religion, but the way the subject
was presented to me: this far-off oriental land, with its
bearded kings, dressed in sandals and robes, its women in
baggy trousers, its water-towers, its unleavened bread, its
donkeys and palm trees, its Hebrew names, its circum-
cised males, the gourds attached to the staffs of those
anchorites you could see in the stained-glass windows at
Saint-Philippe-du-Roule, that sad church outside which
well-to-do gentlemen expressed their dissatisfaction with
the government, their shiny *"huit-reflet"* top hats perched
above their walking-sticks, as they poured scorn on the
Jews, without seeing that it was they themselves who were
the true Pharisees.

At the age of seventeen, I opened the window; the air of
the stadium blew in; the springy turf, the cinder tracks, the
mud of the rugby field in which so many statues were
instantaneously sculpted, the diving boards in the rare
swimming-pools, the sound of swords echoing in fencing
halls…. Suddenly, I felt alive! Up until then, I had lived like
a robot assembled by some stranger; I could only escape
this vertical sleepwalking through exercise, and it was
thanks to this that I came to understand that we have only
one life and that we must give it all the attention we can.

Muscular energy stimulated strength of mind; physical
effort and work suddenly became enjoyable; my cavort-
ing found a rhythm; conserving one's breath meant that

I developed a horror of chattering; I learnt that gentleness could go hand in hand with firm muscles; all that education, religious instruction and civic training ought to have taught me, I acquired in a curiously roundabout way through sport; I came to terms with laws and rules, I discovered the collective conscience, a liking for teamwork, and love of one's neighbour, things which nobody had ever spoken to me about. I had only ever seen duty in an abstract, off-putting way; sport allowed me to feel it, to experience it and to love it; I understood that you had to pass the ball.

It doesn't do to be young in France, for this beautiful country does not lend itself to love at first sight; who was there to explain to me how one loved one's country, or even that I had one? I loved my family, my city, my classmates, my neighbourhood, my home; in 1900, my country was the universe. At the time it would have been unthinkable, and even indecent, to have to comment on the good fortune of having been born in France; who, after all, would have considered being born anywhere else? The miraculous survival of the nation over the centuries was something that went without saying, by some divine gift; in any case, *la patrie* had recently given far too much service to the "scoundrels on the General Staff"; the Théâtre-Libre, the Sorbonne and the Naturalist novels were making sure it did not begin again. France was so powerful, so unique, so vast, filling double-pages of the atlases in pink, that she did not need anyone to love her: to love someone was to be afraid for them: this France which the world took under its protection, shored up on her right by the Tsar, resting on the arm of Edward VII on her left, nothing could happen to her; nothing does happen to the rich. Such was the charming ethical nineteenth-century view, when the centre of the universe was the Earth, and that of the planet, Europe, with Paris as its hub; so many nuclei created in order to sustain the pulp of a matchless fruit offered to mankind by God: France.

I realise how astonishing this state of mind may seem today; there was very little miserableness around in 1900. Yesterday, in Geneva, I heard Marcuse[4] denouncing happiness "as objectively reactionary and immoral"; the happiness of the turn of the century, with its three-franc restaurants and its belief in progress, was radical. It was a carefree period, in which no one had a bad conscience, and in which those who suffered did not protest. The word "culpability" was nowhere to be found in the old dictionaries; the Christian-Democrats had scarcely begun to graft social conscience on to the tree of religious remorse. In improving my mind I thought only of enjoying myself, and from the moment I left school each day, this became one and the same thing for me. The nation states scarcely existed then, though they made a pretence of doing so; there was no spider at the centre of the web to mastermind the captive flies; tax collectors wore the blank expression of indirect taxation. Only the Czar required a passport. My days were empty and were not filled with meetings, so no hours were lost. There was space to breathe between people (something unimaginable today when a *Guide to Deserted Villages*—that really takes the biscuit—can be published); there was no "demographic pressure"; political parties were like provincial rallies; no one bothered and there was no commitment; high-rise flats and public examinations were still a thing of the future. Time was unimportant, wealth was not measured, it was like sunshine or oxygen. Our currency retained its purchasing power, which only began to slide after 1918, a date when the government was controlled by Treasury executives; ever since then, by a curious coincidence, it has not stopped dwindling. Earning money meant you had to spend money, talking about money was ill-mannered. My father was considered to be "comfortably off"; this was due to the fact that he had no needs; "it's easier to do without things than to waste time acquiring them", he liked to say; his only riches being a small Breughel, a tiny *Trouville* by Boudin, a Renoir *Head*, and a *Crozant* by Guillaumin. Eugène Morand never entered a bank, and if he needed a pair of shoes, he wrote to Noren, his bootmakers in the rue Pierre-Charon;[5] every year, Jamet, his tailor in the rue Royale would send him, without a fitting, the same navy-blue serge suit; my father roamed tirelessly around Paris on foot, leaving the hired coupé known as the SENSATION to my mother; he never had a penny on him; occasionally, in the evening, I would hear him say to my mother: "I'm going to the Opéra, in Mme Greffulhe's box; put some money (he never counted in *louis d'or*, that was mundane) in my waistcoat pocket, in case she asks me to take her to supper at Paillard's."

In Padua there is a very old mansion, dating from 1256, which is still known as the *Palazzo degli Anziani*: it is the very image of my adolescence; I lived in the past; I dwelt among people from a bygone age; I even went so far as to view the world through the eyes of the "Ancestors". I confided in my father: "When I gaze at the setting sun my sunsets are those of Turner; my clouds are Courbet's skies, my ceilings those of Tiepolo; I can visualise no other thaws than those in paintings by Monet, and all my women have the belly of a Rodin or the legs of a Maillol; I should like to be able to take delight in a pink rose next to a green one, without having to thank Matisse; here we are at Saint-Séverin: I am unable to see it through my own eyes, I need those of your Huysmans. Where do I fit into all this?"

The famous generation gap never struck me as being hard to bridge, such was the natural understanding between my parents and myself, such the pleasure I took in following them along paths they never sought to impose upon me. Their pace of life was my own; when we were travelling, we would spend hours and days, sitting side by side on deck-chairs, not attempting to make contact with the other hotel guests, and understanding one another without the need to speak. I was still out of touch with my own times; what I was experiencing was the world of my family, the air that I breathed was theirs.

Everything was owed to the Ancients, without one ever being able to match them; firstly, one owed them gratitude: I had always noticed my father avoiding walking on the Persian rug in the studio, out of respect for an object from the Middle Ages: "This rug has been handed down to me, I have a duty towards it", he would say. Beauty alone mattered; exactly the reverse of modern times, when beauty will remain exiled until a man hungers for it once more.

I was responsible only to myself, without having any attachments or duties apart from very close blood ties. On my father's side there was nobody left; I had no dead to mourn, no dead to share my life. My mother came from a family of pedigree bourgeoisie, from whom her love for her husband had drawn her apart, but who retained their position; once a week, to preserve the convention, I would go to Sunday dinner at my maternal grandmother's house in the rue Marignan.(I can see the ritual still: decanted bottles of claret, with little heart-shaped pieces of filter paper around the neck of each carafe, on which you could read the growth and the vintage; fruit bowls heaped with cherries and strawberries, with not a single stalk showing; a few adages continue to hover in my memory such as: "It's better reheated the next day.") This section of my family populated the Cour des Comptes[6] with advisers, instructors and auditors: it was the provinces, but in Paris. I discovered the true Paris at our home; here people were classified only by their talents or their originality. On Wednesdays during the winter, there were dinner parties at home; I can see my father, as slim as a Valois, with his curled moustache and the ribbon of his monocle dangling against his starched dinner shirt. "Everybody should sit where they want" was the rule. Members of the Société des Artistes français and of the Institut were abhorred, exceptions being made for Gounod, Pierné and Massenet, who had composed the music for *Drames sacrés* (1893), *Izeÿl* (1894) and other plays written by my father, as well as *Grisélidis* (1891), a neo-medieval mystery play, which had been a triumph for Bartet at the Comédie-Française and which in 1901 was made into a comic opera, with music by Massenet.

Certain Wednesdays were reserved for Italian music: Tosti, a sort of blue-eyed Prince of Wales, who wrote waltzes and ballads that were popular all over Europe, or the composer Isidore de Lara, a good-natured giant of a man, who came with Litvinne or Héglon, or with the celebrated tenor Tamagno; after dinner they made the glass cupboard in the studio vibrate with a song from *Messaline*, the libretto for which had been written by my father and Armand Silvestre:

> *Viens aimer les nuits sont trop brèves,*
> *Viens rêver les jours sont trop courts…*[7]

In Auguste Rodin's case, he would only come to lunch (from about 1903–1908); peeping out of his yellow-white beard, his priapic nose seemed to me to emerge from his pubis; I would see his faun's ears rising from above a mass of spindle trees in our garden, the earthly paradise of the marble depot, on the Quai d'Orsay; ever since 1880, the sculptor had had his studio there, lent to him by the State; we used to live in an adorable little house in the rue de l'Université; here Rodin found shelter from Camille Claudel's demented screams and from the reproaches of Rose, who waited for him every evening at Meudon; this domestic hell was his true *Porte de l'Enfer*, the vast grey, dusty plaster maquette of which I can still see, in his studio, along with his *Ugolin* or his *Enfant prodigue*, which hung, untouched for a quarter of a century, from the

Comtesse Greffulhe

double-doors, covered with spiders' webs. The Rodin of the early years was already a distant figure; the one who took his leave, after lunch, would return to his studio, where Isadora Duncan, or those Americans who queued to have their bust sculpted at a cost of forty thousand gold francs, awaited him. I did not see Rodin again until July 1914, in London; he had come over for the day to open an exhibition, accompanied by the Comtesse Greffulhe; caught off guard by the mobilization, and with the ferry service interrupted, he had been obliged to spend the night there, without any underwear, he was wrapped up in two of the Comtesse's nightdresses, looking very "Guermantes", the sleeves tied about his Praxitelean chest.

THE RHÔNE VALLEY, 1906

THAT MORNING everything was frozen: the landscape, the sun, the sky, the hotel, mankind itself, at one in the ecstasy of no longer being merely a fragment of solidified joy, burning with cold; the swans, which had fallen asleep, awoke with their webbed feet cleft to the ice. So winter was not just sitting with one's feet up, chilblains and stiff ears, but something which had been hidden from me until now: a sort of white summer, but so barren and unproductive that it was in total contrast to the other summer, which was alive with streams and harvests. The word hibernation did not yet exist for me, but I sensed already that the cold ensured a long life; on the thermometer the mercury had disappeared and had taken refuge in its little glass bulb; all that was left of the deciduous trees was their outline; the branches were nothing but airborne roots. I yearned for high places; for the life of a mountain guide, a timber sawyer, a botanist or a cowhand, anything, rather than going back down into the valley. I have never ever forgotten that sudden experience of the universal. Never had I existed so fully. What plenitude! I felt overcome with a simple joy; nothing other than complete harmony with nature, with the world and with the order of things. Now that I was certain that a single moment could be motionless, there was nothing else that I wanted; in a flash, I realised that true riches are priceless.

Much later, I would understand my wonderment at

beholding these virgin peaks; thanks to them, I could escape from a prison; but what was this prison?

I had been brought up in the grimy Paris of Zola, along the tar-blacked streets of Whistler, among Maupassant's gloomy peasants, in Flaubert's sombre countryside, surrounded by hot-air stoves; and, all of a sudden, everything was white! This magical mirror enabled me to glimpse my future life; elemental forces which had hitherto been dormant radiated forth. In a trice, I was at the heart of my being.

Opposite me, on the frontier of Savoy, were sheer ridges that were repelling the North with all their might; at my feet was the blue vapour of the lake, nestling against the Jura, that long snake-like spine, scaled with ice and fir forests; to my right, the terraced promontories of Vevey, Clarens and La Tour, their headlands plunging into the water below which sparkled in the sunlight; behind me were Les Avants, Sonloup and Jaman, their brecciated steps sloping away, snatching up their crumbling soils in order to hurl them into the Rhône, despite the efforts of the chalets and the stony spurs to cling to the horizontal.

Did I know what threatening footsteps I was trying to escape from? Running away, but to do what? To do nothing. I can recognize this wild indolence among young people today; recent surveys among sixteen-year-old boys confirm that, for them, leisure comes before food, where they live, or household appliances.... That day, I was already experiencing what they would feel later, in their millions; I was so light-headed that I felt I could fly away from the thick soup of smoke that stifled the Rhône valley and polluted the lake.

My indecisive character gave way to a resounding faith: I would escape; I did not know what I would do, but I could sense that my life would veer towards abroad, towards elsewhere, towards the light; not tomorrow, immediately; which explains this readiness to seize the moment and this haste of a man in a hurry that have been with me for so long; to escape from man was to escape from Time; I could feel an animal power within me which death alone would cure. "You're a brute", Giraudoux used to tell me. At the same time there began that beat of a pendulum whose rhythm has never left me, a liking for drawing closer, that is in contrast to this passion for space that was ushered in by puberty; the happiness that living in a narrow bedroom gives as opposed to the intoxication of the desert, the sea and the steppes.

I loathed doors and enclosures; frontiers and walls offended me.

ITALY, 1907

WHEN I RAN AWAY for the first time, not yet twenty years old, I threw myself upon Italy as if on the body of a woman. At Cap-Martin, my grandmother encouraged me to admire from afar her idol, the Empress Eugénie, as she went out for her walks ("What shoulders!"); I would follow her to the roulette tables at Monte Carlo, managing to get into the gaming-rooms by slipping beneath the balustrade, since I was under the legal age. With four or five gold coins in my pocket, my first and last winnings, I took advantage of a reduction in fares to mark the opening of the recently completed Simplon tunnel, and I set off for Naples to meet the Italian steamship on which Giraudoux was sailing, as he arrived back from Harvard.

At Naples I would rediscover the same physical and moral euphoria I had experienced at Caux; it was during a solitary lunch beneath an arbour, above San Elmo; I watched as the sounds of men working rose up from below me. There was nothing happening, I was expecting nothing, I was giving nothing, and yet I was receiving everything. Millions of years had stood in wait in order to offer me this sublime gift: a morning beneath an arbour. There was no reason why this should not continue. A tradition of very long standing ensured that everything, myself included, had a predestined place. I was embarking on life intending to obtain what was my due: Titian and Veronese, who had only painted in order to be admired by me, awaited me; Italy had been preparing for my visit for centuries.

It seemed to me only natural to reap what others had sown. High above the lines of washing that draped the Neapolitan streets, I floated in the unreality of a sky that gulped in the smoky fumes of Vesuvius. This detachment, this contemplative egoism and this passivity did not spare me from boredom; short-cuts have very much extended my travels, even if laziness has lengthened my life. I flitted about among people, I fluttered around things, I ricocheted off hard surfaces, fleeing all attachments, somewhat unsure of my feelings and entirely devoted to myself. A fervent pilgrim, I was dazzled by everything. "I shall have to return to France, UNFORTUNATELY" reads a postcard I came across, sent to my mother at the time. Later on, I used to feel ashamed about such things, up until the day last year when my eye fell upon an interview with the year's top student at the Centrale[8] in Le Figaro, and I read the following: "Your plans for the future?" "I'm leaving to spend a year in the United States, at Berkeley University." "And afterwards?" "After that… France, UNFORTUNATELY." Yesterday's blasphemy is an everyday remark nowadays. My offspring agreeing with me, sixty years later.

LOMBARDY, 1908

DISCOVERING NAPLES was like giving the sun its real name; living in Lombardy, there to await our entry into the Veneto, was something entirely different, it was like the transition from friendship to love.

In the summer, my parents descended upon Italy as if they were visiting the Holy Land, ready to receive the Law there. It was a world of museums, art galleries and libraries, among which could be found certain buildings that served the public—factories, railway stations, or farms—necessary for life's commodities. On our travels we encountered a different kind of humanity, one which spoke in a strange language that was to do with insolvencies, profits, strikes, salaries and yield per hectare. All these were meaningless to us.

We spent a few weeks at Tremezzo, where the lake was flecked with water-lily leaves. In these summer gardens, stretched out under the shade of magnolia trees with their lemon-scented flowers, we followed in the footsteps of Milanese cardinals who had walked here since the sixteenth century; by Lake Como we awaited the end of the Canicula, of those days of hellish heat, which in Lombardy, along the shores of the Po, cause even the leaves of the willows to become scorched.

One day I set off from Tremezzo to Bellagio, swimming the two kilometres along the lake through water so viscous that as I moved through it I felt as if I were stroking a fish.

During the last days of August, I took refuge in the chestnut groves of the Tremezzina, which were as chill as a marble by Thorvaldsen; I can see myself in the slow train that brought me back from some trip to the Ticino where I had gone to stock up with cigarettes, looking down upon the wonderfully phosphorescent stars formed by the chestnut blossom. I have never forgotten the smell of that chestnut grove in the Tremezzina, the same forest that Fabrice crossed[9] on his way to Waterloo. It was in Tremezzo that I acquired a liking for chestnuts, for those wonderful hedgehogs, and for the tree's sickle-like leaves. I was to live in a chestnut grove again in 1944; in Montreux, for three years, I lived off chestnuts that had been piled up, their burrs still on, in a bath that had fallen into disuse because the gas bills had not been paid; the chestnut grove of *"Maryland"* sloped down from the deserted villa as far as the first roofs of Territet, before disappearing into Lake Geneva; chestnut trees like those which *La Nouvelle Héloïse* places at Clarens, almost wholly destroyed today to make way for vineyards. As soon as September arrived, we set off for Venice; the surroundings changed; the cypress trees by Lake Como gave way to the factory chimneys of the Lombardy plain; all along the railway lines the vines were no longer being cut by hand; from the carriage window, Milan was paving the way for a new industrial Italy; what was the point of so many tyres, ball-bearings and idiotic industries? I lived with my back turned to the future; could the future be anything other than an immanent past?

A stop-over in Milan; in those days the favourite hotel

of French visitors was the Albergo di Francia; my father walked into the bedroom; standing on the chimney-piece was a hideous group of bronze statues decorating the top of an Italian clock of the worst Victor-Emmanuel I period: "I could never get to sleep in the presence of such a horror! Let's be on our way!" my father exclaimed. So we set off again for Venice, without eating or sleeping. It wasn't a pose: my father was a true product of the age of Ruskin; he had known William Morris and the Pre-Raphaelites, and the concept of *liberty*, which invested the most everyday object with the dignity of a work of art; for him, putting up with ugliness in our home was to sully oneself. I have seen Lalique, adopting Tolstoy's example, sewing slippers for himself, and Gallé building his own ovens, as did later Brancusi, who cooked steaks for us in them. My father designed the costumes and the scenery for his plays; he even painted a medieval stage curtain, in the style of Burne-Jones, for the Comédie Française.

1908
VENICE SEEN THROUGH A
REAR-VIEW MIRROR

Venice, which Proust called "the Mecca of the religion of Beauty". Eight years earlier, Proust, whom I did not know at the time (although my father used to meet him at Madeleine Lemaire's, as I would discover from Proust himself ten years later) had seen Venice through Ruskin's eyes, but already he was aware how exacting this religion of Beauty was. "Ruskin did not conceive of Beauty as an object of pleasure, but as a reality that was more important than life...." Had Proust stopped at *Jean Santeuil*, he would have been nothing more than a hedonist; but he suffered, he searched beyond Beauty, he produced *Swann*. This is why our stern age forgives him for his duchesses. Naïve and foolish, it never occurred to me that we have duties towards Beauty; for me, she was just a way of evading the moral code; and Ruskin, as Bloch says, was a frightful bore.

I can hear myself saying and repeating: "You deny the past, you reject the present, you are hurtling towards a future that you will not see." I want to speak plainly; this is why, overcoming my dislike of myself, I have taken Venice as my confidante; she will answer for me. In Venice I can think about my life, and do so more clearly than anywhere else; and it's too bad if I can be spotted in the corner of the picture, like Veronese in *Christ in the House of Levi*.

The canals of Venice are black as ink; it is the ink of

Marcel Proust in Venice

Jean-Jacques, of Chateaubriand, of Barrès, of Proust; to dip one's pen into it is more than a Frenchman's duty, it is a duty plain and simple.

Venice did not withstand Attila, Bonaparte, the Hapsburgs, or Eisenhower; she had something more important to do: survive; they believed they were building upon rock; she sided with the poets and decided to be built on water.

I have always thought of the railway station at Venice as a triumphal entrance; at that time it was not the present-day peristylar railway theatre of the Mussolini era. ("This is Venice, Venezia, Venedig: you'll see what you shall see. *Viva il Duce!*") Its predecessor consisted of three arcades which had turned green from the damp and had been blackened by the coal smoke. What has not changed is the green copper dome of San Simeone Piccolo; the bombs of two world wars, aimed at the railways lines, had spared it; to the left and in front of it are the *trattorie* where you dine, your head beneath the boxed bay trees and your feet in the water; there is less of a stench from the waters of these Fondamente Santa Lucia or dei Turchi than elsewhere; propelled through, the water is oxygenated here and does not give off the whiff of sulphurous hydrogen.

In those days, the gondolier was still king; proud at having surprised us by taking the short cut along the Rio Nuovo upon leaving the station and emerging suddenly at the ACCADEMIA, our man, manipulating his curved oar like a foil, reeled off the dazzling names of the *palazzi*: FOSCARI, GIUSTINIANI, REZZONICO, LOREDAN, VENIER,

DARIO... (Some of them, bent over with age and rheumatic stress, looked as if they were bowing at us.) Along the way, the gondolier, hostile still to the outboard engine, cocked a snook at the steamships that passed. Only yesterday, the *vaporetti*, the masters of the canals, had gone on strike to prevent the last of the gondolas from using the Rio Nuovo; the calm waters has been replaced by constant rough waves.[10]

At last we arrived within sight of the Dogana with its statue of Fortune on top, which, at that time, was golden; today Fortune has turned verdigris.[11]

This triumphant procession along the Grand Canal, "that register of Venetian nobility", as Théophile Gautier put it, led us to the Traghetto San Maurizio, where the small apartment rented by my parents awaited us. The narrow street was deserted; there was just a basket which, at the cry of "*Bella uva!*" (fine grapes), had been lowered on a rope down to the grape-seller below, and hoisted up again piled with muscat grapes for the lunch that had already been served. The mosquito nets had been folded parachute fashion above the beds, and the bedrooms smelled of dead gnats, killed by little triangles of beguiling but nauseating herbs; from the canal there rose up a reek of foul water, similar to the smell of vases from which someone has forgotten to remove the withered flowers.

In the morning, I was awoken by the hoarse voice of the *vaporetto* and by the striated reflections from the Canal on the almond green ceiling, with its plaster reliefs, or on the façades of the buildings that were flecked with light; for fifty centimes, the barber would come up and trim my beard (a marvellous attack on the bristles by the Italian razors, engraved in gold on steel, which each barber carried with him on weekdays). Nowadays, when I go around barefoot in espadrilles and without a tie all year round, I sometimes smile when I think of how I was attired at that time: white flannel trousers, white cotton socks, white felt hat, a butterfly knot and a stiff collar.

The *rampino* from the San Maurizio ferry greeted me with a cry of *poppe*!, waving his grubby hat (even poor people wore a hat; a hat they used to greet one with) as he held the gondola's coupling hook with his other hand. He offered to carry me across the Canal, rather as Dandolo's Serenissima offered to take the Crusaders as far as Byzantium. I did not make use of his services, but set off along the narrow street towards the Palazzo Pisani (painted at that time in that pale nacreous "coral" pink, the colour of scampi); I reached the Palazzo Morosini with its lofty ogives, and so Gothic in style that it looked English. Passing the churches of Santa Maria Zobenigo, San Stefano and San Vitale, I was on my way to meet my mother, after she had attended Mass, at San Moisè, whose façade, an assortment of overhangs and recesses, was white with the acidic droppings of the Venetian pigeons that can even eat into the stonework. Théophile Gautier was responsible for my love of this church, which, with its obelisks and astragals, is so perfectly reminiscent of the overture to Rossini's *Moisè*. I drew back the red curtain (the same one as today, without those horrible doors with bars): there were more votive candles burning inside than in the Holy Sepulchre; the Jesuits' confessional boxes,

Théophile Gautier photographed by Paul Nadar

their baroque grilles as convoluted as a *confiteor*, buzzed with the whisper of sins; confessional boxes only came into existence, apparently, in the seventeenth century; that buttoned up age was the first to feel that it should conceal its sins … I enjoyed stopping in front of the tomb of a Scotsman, John Law, the inventor of the banknote; this rococo monument was an apt one for the inventor of financial rococo (inflation is romantic, while deflation is classical).

"If Palférine had any money, he would spend his life in Venice, passing his days in museums, his evenings at the theatre, and his nights with beautiful women" (*Balzac*). The Fenice was not open; as for beautiful women, I was too frightened of imitating Jean-Jacques [Rousseau], who found little consolation in his loneliness from a courtesan who almost got him plastered, from another tart who only had one nipple, or from the young girl of twelve who was so sexually immature that he contented himself with fatherly affection and teaching her music. Depriving one-self of women was painful in the evenings, but I would never have dared approach, as President De Brosses did after consulting the *Tariffa delle putane di Venezia*, the Mari-anna or Fornarina of a republic of demi-beavers.

Deprived! This word has no meaning for our children or for their impetuous age, which imposes no restraints on passions or on the insistence of desire; the young of today have the voracious weakness of unbridled crowds. It was this abstinence of the flesh that gave us a self-control that is rarely seen any longer; it was not until about 1920, when we decided that we were being deprived and that we would fast no longer, that we began to fling ourselves upon easy prey, whose fragrance lost in subtlety what it gained in abundance. Virgins, nowadays, await their boy-friends in their beds; in the early part of the century, all we had were prostitutes, and even then one had to be able to gain access to the brothel; that depended on the height of the client; the first of our classmates to be allowed inside was Baudelocque—the son of the well-known obstetrician—who was two heads taller than us; while waiting for him, we would plod up and down the pavement of the rue de Hanovre; when he came out, the questions rained down: "What does she look like, a woman?" "You enter her? How's that possible!" We were thirteen years old; we would still have to wait a while.... Today, I miss the old days and the time one spent wait-ing; the penitence and the continence that society imposed on us imparted an unbelievable flavour to the opposite sex, and they conferred something sacred that has been lost. It was still the Italy of the young Beyle, and of his "two years without a woman"; he wanted to remedy this: aged eighteen, he contracted syphilis.

As to the young ladies (whom at that time one did not refer to as "girls"), one was expected to make amends.

In those days, boys made amends, they took responsi-bility for anything that went wrong: compensation and penitence; it was all to do with the feudal code of honour, with Corsican revenge, with civil action. A young lady must not be *compromised*, a terrible word that suggested commit-ment, shady deals and law suits; having an illegitimate child was like contracting the most shameful of diseases. It was no laughing matter. Traps lay everywhere; in every invitation, even on the simplest of promenades the female body offered its stumbling-blocks; charms were lures; at the bottom of the slope of the thighs, so sweet a descent, lay the pot of glue.

I can still see my school friend Robert D., sitting astride one of the porphyry lions in St Mark's Square, telling me how he had had a narrow escape:

"I met her yesterday, in front of one of the Bellinis at the Accademia; I got rid of the mother and the sister. We agreed to meet this morning. I went to collect her at the Danieli."

"Mademoiselle is not quite ready; she asks you to go up …"

"I find her dressed, wearing a broad-brimmed hat with cherries on top, with an embroidered parasol and a silk scarf round her neck. My dear, imagine the bedroom, with its smell of crumpled sheets, cold coffee and warm soap … I sit down beside her …"

"On the sofa?"

"Far worse! On the counterpane…. My head is spinning. I start to stammer: 'Your mother might come in …' Impossible to finish my sentence, I couldn't bear it any longer; every passing second made me want to curl up and die."

"What can the tributary do when it encounters the river, apart from lose itself? So you're engaged, congratulations."

"… Her arms were encircling my neck, like a ring around this finger; her handcuffs …"

" … Her handcuffs?"

"Her breasts pressed against my chest; her stomach took on a strange life of its own, and there were convulsions, as if she were in labour …"

"You're cutting corners!"

"Her elder sister walked in, with a curious look on her face, which expressed everything, envy, disgust, complicity … everything except naturalness.… Just then, through the open window, beneath the Ponte della Paglia, I saw a gondolier pass by; '*Oi*' he shouted. You know what that means in gondoliers' language: *Watch out*! It did not fall on deaf ears."

Listening to Robert D., I swore that I would never become a lover.

I was extremely shy in the company of married women; if the initiative came from them, my mother's sighs would grow increasingly unsubtle and her entreaties more frequent. Nowadays, that also raises a smile; every age has its misfortunes.

Adorned with rings and cooing like the pigeons of St Mark's, the pederasts strutted past; Venice, "an unnatural city" (*Chateaubriand*), had always welcomed them; I spotted one of them there, a man who had become so well-known on account of a recent trial that we would point him out to one another as he was leaving the Carnot; it was the famous Fersen, who had just published a poem about Venice, Notre-Dame des Cendres. "I do not shake hands with pederasts", my father would say (never suspecting that he was doing so all day long). "Yet another of those gentlemen of the cuff", he would add (at the time, they could be recognized by the handkerchief issuing from their cuffs). The inverts, "that outcast section of the human community" as an unpublished letter of Proust's puts it, constituted a secret society; one cannot appreciate *Temps perdu* unless one remembers that in those days Sodom represented a curse. Even in Venice, homosexuality was nothing more than the most subtle of the fine arts.

With a canvas under one arm, his box of paints under the other and his easel on his back, in the tradition of Monsieur Courbet, my father crossed the waters and installed himself on the steps of the Salute, opposite the Abbey of San Gregorio; as a young man, he had rented this abbey, nowadays an American's luxury pied-à-terre, but which at that time was in ruins; he dabbed his thumb in his palette and ground his knife on the rough cast of the walls. All painters have loved the votive basilica of the Salute; Guardi, Canaletto, the romantics and the impressionists, none has been able to resist the curve of its unfurled scrolls that resemble waves about to break, lured by the play of the sunlight around the grey-green dome, whose sphere reflects every nuance of broken colour.

The French in Venice used to meet in St Mark's Square, having dined in their modest lodging-house, or princely dining-room, glad to have escaped from some titled hostess or other; some came from the Palazzo Dario, "bent over, like a courtesan, beneath the weight of her necklaces" (people adored D'Annunzio!); others from the Palazzo Polignac, or the Palazzo Da Mula, bringing with them from the house of Contessa Morosini (who dared to wear a doge's hat) the latest news from the Court

Gabriele D'Annunzio at the regatta on Lake Garda, 1930

at Berlin, for which the Mula acted as a sounding-board. We would drink *granite*, coffee with crushed ice, in the company of Mariano Fortuny, the son of the Spanish Meissonier, who had become a Venetian by adoption, the interior decorator Francis Lobre and his wife, who was physician to Anna de Noailles (a famous name at that time), the designer Drésa, and Rouché, not yet in charge of the Opéra, who was editor of the *Grande Revue*, which launched Maxime Dethomas and Giraudoux; then there was André Doderet, who by dint of translating D'Annunzio had come to look like him; we would be joined by several officials from the École des Beaux-Arts, colleagues of my father: Roujon, Havard, Henry Marcel (Gabriel's father), the head of the Beaux-Arts, the Baschet brothers and Roger Marx (father of Claude).

These were real people, not international stars like those who would invade Venice later on, at the time of the Ballets Russes; this circle of friends was discreet, as French people were at that time; they were extremely fussy men, encyclopaedic in their knowledge, highly influential, very sure in their tastes, modest to a degree and disdainful of fashions, who talked with an inimitable accent, and no one "pulled the wool over their eyes". None of them was garish, or popped the corks of champagne bottles, or motored about on the Lagoon making waves; there were no "relationships"; their wives' necklaces were made of Murano glass.

They loathed all things commercial, and in Venice more so than elsewhere; this was reflected in the frightful Salviati shop, with its one thousand chandeliers that were

lit in broad daylight, which still disfigures the Grand
Canal to this day. They owned a few drawings by old
masters, but not paintings (they had not the means); they
were not theorists or intellectuals, their words did not end
in *isme*; one could extend the list indefinitely of what they
were not, of what they did not say or do, and yet they did
not resemble anyone else; unlike people in society they
did not talk for the sake of talking; the other day I heard
someone admiring Léautaud's free spirit, as if it were
something odd; through his outspokenness, his culture
and independence, each of these delightful fellows from
the days of my youth was the equal of Léautaud; they
seemed quite ordinary to me, for I had no one to compare them with; nowadays I realize that they represented
more than Culture, they were Civilization.

They may not have known what they wanted, but they
knew very precisely what they did not want; they might
have forgiven a Ravachol;[12] but bores (the word they
used was "*mufles*") never; like Jules Renard, they had very
definite dislikes. None of them was mediocre (I only discovered mediocrity later on, in the Civil Service). Their
remarks constituted a sort of *santa conversazione*. I can still
picture the way they looked: black alpaca, black bamboo
boater, grey cotton gloves, a white piqué cravat in summer, black crêpe-de-chine necktie in winter; starched
shirt with stiff collar and cuffs; the *vaporetti* they called *hiron-
delles*, or *pyroscaphes*, or *mouches*; to save money, they went to
read *Le Figaro* in the offices of the Querini-Stampalia
Foundation; they never forgave Napoleon's architects for
the destruction of the exquisite San Giminiano church,

built by Sansovino, at the entrance to the Procuraties; and they blazed with fury about that Palladio who had wanted to pull down St Mark's in order to replace it with a neo-classical temple.

Politics did not exist for them. How distant was the Dreyfus affair already…. Politics was something that had disappeared since the time of Loubet[13] (1900); it would surface again until 1936. For them, Barrès was still the anarchist of his early novels, and Maurras was merely a poet; Boulanger, Dreyfus and Déroulède were champions of a sport that was outmoded, that of politics. They would scarcely have been able to name the Président du Conseil of the time; the Ancien Régime for them was neither Turgot, nor the Abbé Terray; it was Gouthière,[14] or Gabriel; they did not say: "France regained a colonial empire under Vergennes", but: "The bronzes have never been so well gilded as they were under Louis XVI." They did not use the royal dynasties as reference points; the reigns that counted for them were those of Goya or Delacroix. Their Venice was still that of 1850, that of Théophile Gautier, the Salute and its "population of statues", and the flaking mosaics.

I would come across them at our table, at home, seated around a perfect risotto, creamy with parmesan, or in front of a plateful of eels from the *Laguna morta*, grilled over a wood fire and dripping with garlic butter. Constantly smiling, but never laughing, my father was somewhat eclipsed by his so colourful guests. The past, for them, was the present; Armand Baschet, one of the first Casanova scholars, would announce the recent discovery of letters written by women at the Bohemian castle of Dux: "They thought Casanova was a braggart? He scarcely told the whole truth!" For me, Casanova was a bit like some disreputable uncle. Camille Mauclair would arrive for coffee; there would be an argument about which room Musset had occupied at the Danieli, formerly the Albergo Reale; was it number thirteen, as Louise Colet claimed, or the two rooms mentioned by Pagello? Emotions eclipsed cultural considerations: the Doges' Palace was all very well, but should one not regret the old palace, the Byzantine one, with its drawbridge and its watch-towers that dated from the year 1000, on the site of a *piazzetta* which was then a port? The Venetian balustered bridges made of marble are certainly charming, but imagine those that preceded them, gently sloping and without railings, over which the procurators rode on horseback, leaving their mounts to eat hay afterwards on the Ponte della Paglia. Thus did our friends hark back to the past, rather like the trout that swims upstream and jumps the weir to obtain more oxygen.

The painter Toché, a character who had remained typical of the MacMahon[15] era, used to ring our door-bell at the grappa hour; he continued to paint frescoes in the style in which they had been painted in Venice three centuries earlier; Toché was famous for having decorated the Chabanais in tempera; he had worked for a year, without setting foot outside this brothel, famous for its Edward VII room, and mixed quite openly with *le Tout-Paris* in this place of ill repute (at the Beaux-Arts, Toché was known by his pupils as Pubis de Chabanais); a good-looking man, he had seduced the owner of Chenonceaux and persuaded her to give Venetian festivals there—with gondolas brought over from the *piazzetta*—which Emilio Terry, the next owner, still remembered having seen in his youth, rotting beneath the arches over the River Cher. "I paint only at night", Toché used to say; "Venice by day, I leave to Ziem!" After which, he would walk down our staircase humming some *Ombra adorata* of Crescentini's (like the singer Genovese, in his *C major* so dear to Balzac), curling his handlebar moustache.

Rather like the doges whose embossed velvet robes he wore at those Persian balls which were all the rage in Paris, Mariano Fortuny, emerging from his studio, would invite us to his mother's house, opposite the miniature *palazzo* which had been rented by the actress Réjane; Mme Fortuny offered us teas that were worthy of Parmesan;[16] her table, which was covered in Venetian crochet work, was a veritable fruit market, repoussé copper plates with peaches alternating with beribboned and gilded assortments of frilly pastries sprinkled with a powdered sugar, for which I have forgotten the Venetian name. Proust had been entertained there, eight years earlier; He had known Fortuny; later on he would provide a great number of dresses designed by this artist for *The Captive*; they have become part of the Proustian legend.

Occasionally, one of my father's pupils would come from Paris at his invitation to join us, and was welcomed at their teacher's home as he or she might have been in Renaissance times; it was the tradition set by Lecoq de Boisbaudran, whom my father had succeeded at the

École des Arts Decoratifs, where the director's office with it's Louis XV panelling was decorated with a portrait of Van Loo, the first patron of the École Royale de Dessin, founded in 1765 by Bachelier, Madame de Pompadour's protector; a vanished race of monocle-wearing *fonction-naires* who kept well away from the management of the École des Beaux-Arts, who were indifferent to honours, had independent minds and advanced tastes, who couldn't care less about the Prix de Rome and medals awarded by the jury, and who were opposed to the Institut; for those at the Quai Malaquais,[17] Lecoq was "the accursed teacher" and the Arts Decoratifs the refuge of those whose talents were advanced or insane; Boisbaudran had had Renoir, Rodin, Monet, Degas, Fantin as pupils; my father had: Segonzac, Brianchon, Oudot, Legueult. That's sufficient to commemorate these two men.

My father had Mallarmé's physique: the same haughty profile, the same sharply pointed beard; he sported neither rosette nor tie; "a rose, yes, a rosette, no", he used to say, although Jules Renard, in his *Journal*, was indignant that his Cross [of the Légion d'Honneur] should have been taken away from him, because of a promotion, in order for it to be given to my father. He was somewhat defensive in his courteousness, absurdly modest, constrained, self-doubting and admiring only of others; he spent his life tearing up manuscripts and repainting his canvases. When Mallarmé told him: "Even to write is to put black upon white", he wrote no more; appointed as head of a *grande école*, his first utterance was: "I'll be able to learn at last."

Between the Quadri and Florian cafés an entire European society lived out its last days in Venice. And not just the French. Franz-Josef, the old forest tree, would bury them all in his fall. Austrian grandees descended on Venice while waiting for the stags to rut, before taking the road northwards to their dozen or more castles in Styria or the Tyrol; dressed in their *jäger*, their moss-green hats set on hareskin skulls, and loden capes, they left behind them a whiff of Russian leather and the magnolia scent of the Borromée islands, which did their best to imitate Pivert, the perfumer of Napoleon III, whose children were friends of ours. These Austrians, Czernin, Palffy, or Festetics, in their *reisekostüm*, supplied titled Europe with their last stallions: Rocksavage, Howard de Walden and Westminster in London; Beauvau or Quinsonas in France; in Italy, Florio or Villarosa became their patrons, doing their best to match them in indolence, distinction and seduction. In the Procuraties all one could hear was: "I've just arrived from Pommersfelden, from Caprarola, from Arenenberg, from Knole, from Stupinigi, from Huistenbosch, from Kedelston ..." Austria-Hungary was not one nation, but ten; it was the flower of Europe; England, with its lords, who for four centuries had been marrying coal merchants' daughters, could not produce one tenth of the degrees of descent of the Austrian nobility; Bismarck's Germany, enriched by the famous Jews who had made it wealthy, Italy, still trembling in the shadow of Rakowsky, and the Balkan nations, who came to Vienna to make up their minds about what Norpois would have called "the favoured of the Salon Bleu", all had eyes only for Austria; Venice lived beneath the floodlights of the white steamships of Austrian Lloyd, the masters of the Adriatic, and it was Strauss whose tunes were still requested in the evenings, when we paced up and down the quadrangle of St Mark's. Venice virtually belonged to these Austrians, through the Triplice, the triple alliance of Italy with Vienna and Berlin. Was not Bonaparte, at Campo Formio, the first to make Austria a present of Venice, in spite of the orders of the Directoire?

1909

I̶N THE AUTUMN of 1909, my heart in a fury, I left
Venice, taking with me to my regiment an old eighteenth
century guide-book, *Les Délices de l'Italie,* by Rogissart,
whose steel-plate engravings depicted a virtually deserted
Venice in which, hidden in the corner of the *campi,* were
some rare masks to provide scale. Even when I was under
fire during the war, at the mouth of the River Orne, I
thought of nothing but that of the Brenta.

After a period serving in the countryside, sheltering in
an old house in the rue de l'Engannerie, where I had
rented a squaddie's room, I started to write a Venetian
play, that was inspired by my reading the *Lettres à Sophie
Volland*: under pain of death it was forbidden for senators
of the Serenissima to sleep with foreign representatives; a
senator who was smitten had no other means of meeting
his beloved than to traverse the French ambassador's
house; caught off guard and denounced, my hero chose
decapitation rather than admit to a secret tryst; romanticism was not dead.... I had hung above my bed the first
map of the world, dating from 1457, a reproduction of Fra
Mauro's planisphere, and the map of Venice drawn by
Jacopo Barbari in 1500. My heart had remained in
Venice. I was envious of my Oxford friends, who were able
to go back there without me; I compared my fate to theirs;
the Channel relieved them of this duty to serve their country for two years; was not a European war unthinkable?
Every single mental impulse carried me away from the

barracks far from frontiers; I read *The Times*, or *Les Conversations avec Eckermann* in the mess-room, after roll-call, by the light of a candle stuck on to a bayonet. At the library in Caen, where I had just been appointed an auxiliary, I launched myself on the early travellers in Italy; I made some astounding discoveries; when I was young, no one had direct access to works of quality, you had to discover them and deserve them; there were no Carpaccios for sale on Uniprix calendars; liking Giorgione or Crivelli meant being introduced into any number of small secret societies; Antonello da Messina was a sort of place of ill repute, whose address was passed around among the initiated.

Instead of boldly accepting the fate that was common to those of my age, I turned my back on chores, vaulting the wall or leaving the barracks at daybreak in order not to have to answer the bugle's call; having to get up at the sound of drums or having to stand stock-still at the blast of a whistle were like a slap across the face for me.

A little patience: the unpleasant young man would change his stripes; not immediately; it would only be at the end of his life that he would go to school; the way in which you fetch up in a certain period matters less than the period you are leaving behind; life is a slow business, a two-fold process, luck and oneself; that's what gives a work its shape.

In the meantime, I was like the young Buddha whose family concealed the existence of death to him until he was thirty.

I was a very old gentleman, a little too dyed in the wool, but delighted to be so.

CAEN, 1910

A T THE ARCHIVES department of the Préfecture, Major Jaquet made me copy out lists of volunteers from Calvados in 1792; beneath the folders I concealed Fabert, Dupaty, De Brosses, La Lande, Amelot de La Houssaye, all those, in short, who were lovers of Venice. On the headed paper of the Conseil Général du Calvados, I wrote letters to my friends not unlike the following, which I recently came across; it is easy to see the extent to which Venice continued to matter to me:

From the Archives of the Générallité
Caen.
This Thursday 27th of October 176…

I have received from you, Abbé, a letter from Vicenza, informing me that you are already nearing Venice. A glance at the envelope, which the mail orderly of the Royal Normandy *has delivered to me, and which bears the arms of the République, tells me that your journey has ended at last. Shall you come from Padua as the crow flies, by barge, or will you stop to visit a few friends on the Brenta? I had been affeared at the prospect of a disagreeable stay in the lazaretto for you, since there is cholera in the Duchy of Parma and in Lombardy; but I see that nothing has come of it. Are your rags and tatters at Scomparini's house? And you yourself?*

I trust, Abbé, that you are not bored to distraction in the absence of the two gentle ladies from Florence, whom we were accustomed to stroke and kiss last year?

Did you know that there are fifty-one references to Venice in

Shakespeare, even though he never left England? At least this is what
H.F. Brown maintains in his Studies in the History of Venice,
which he published last year with Murray's.

Saia sends you her kindest regards. We often reread the satires of
Aretino, Mensius and Portier des Chartreux together. So vouchsafe
to send me by the hand of our mutual friend, the Nuncio, a few
aphrodisiac tablets which, so Juvenal says:

arouse desire as if by hand.

I envy you your travels; what with some Orvieto, a discreet casino
at Murano, a nun with perfumed breasts and a letter of exchange
payable at Milord Cook's, there are no sad thoughts in Venice.

Farewell Abbé. I am strongly tempted to sell my commission to
the army and leave by the next coach to join you.

P.S.—Do you like the epigram I have composed in the style of
Martial, about Saia, who is unfaithful to me?

Candidior farina cutis,
Communior mola corpus.
"Your skin is whiter than flour
Your body more banal than a mill."

Is it Latin?
(Late 1910)

And here is another letter, still in mock-scholarly vein:

The Archives
Caen
This Thursday the 3rd of November 1910

My Dear Friend,

You are truly the pride of French and Ultramontane clergy; Abbé Galiani should bow low, he has a master! You are piquant, reproving and smutty, but never obscene, even when you are describing the Nuncio's love affairs, "on the other side of the coin". Is la Morosina susceptible to your signals? Why don't you look at her through a telescope, as Lord Queensberry did from his Piccadilly window?

I have been reading a lot lately: Amiel's *Journal*, Italian Women in the Renaissance *by Rodocanachi; the letters of* Pliny, The Dream of Polyphilus, *in a fine 1599 edition, the* Memoirs of the Princesse Palatine, *Müntz's* Vinci, *etc. I have heard very good reports of* The Woollen Dress *by Henry Bordeaux, which has even been compared to Bovary.*

Wednesday 21 June 1911

Another letter, postmarked Caen, 36th Infantry Division, contains this childlike cry: *"My freedom, for G's sake! I feel nostalgic for the universe, I'm homesick for every country!"*

1911

THIS YEAR, all I had to do to remind myself of Venice was to take a look at the famous floods that occurred in Paris in the spring; on leave, I went by boat from Saint-Germain-des Prés to the Champ-de-Mars, by way of the rue de l'Université.

MASTER CORVO

A S I WAS on the point of leaving Venice, one of the
most eccentric of Englishmen had just arrived, that
strange Corvo, whose existence was only disclosed to me
forty years later. I was narrowly to miss, alas, the two most
inexplicable islanders of those days, T.E. Lawrence and
Corvo; in 1917 Georges-Picot, the French High Commis-
sioner in a Holy Land not yet recaptured from the Turks,
had invited me to accompany him to the siege of Jerusalem:
it would have meant my spending over a year in the company of Colonel Lawrence; I turned down the position.

I remain equally upset not to have known Rolfe, who,
during that summer of 1909 when we were both in
Venice, was known as "Baron Corvo"; the poet, Shane
Leslie, who wrote Corvo's epitaph, and with whom I was
on friendly terms, would have been able to introduce us.
Why did he adopt the name "Corvo"? Why that *never
more*? Out of romanticism? Rolfe always loved heraldry;
as a seminarist, he dreamt up coats of arms and devised
banners, and he would walk into the refectory with a
stuffed crow perched on his shoulder. Corvo was a mix-
ture of Léon Bloy and Genet, of Max Jacob and Maurice
Sachs. Poor and lonely in his lifetime, he was unstable
and eccentric in character, as well as being litigious, spite-
ful, devious and vindictive; he had a talent for all the arts;
he was constantly angry with his friends; he read horo-
scopes, and he was intoxicated with the Church's past
and with the Renaissance; he adored Catholic pomp and

ceremony, but he had no vocation for the priesthood and he was expelled from every school, as well as from sinecures, salons and asylums; he let people down, deceiving both Cardinal Vaughan and Hugh Benson, those two pillars of English Catholicism, who were initially attracted to him, but very soon grew exasperated.

A.J.A. Symons in his celebrated *The Quest for Corvo*, a posthumous investigation among all those who had known this character, retraces his life from his time in the seminary up until his time in Venice. Master Corvo must have been unable to find anywhere to perch in this city without trees. In that summer of 1909, Corvo stayed at the Hotel Bellevue, paid for by his friend, Professor Dawkins.

A member of the Bucintoro sailing club, Corvo actually learned to steer a gondola, a highly difficult skill at which I have only seen a woman, Winnaretta de P., excel, for a misdirected blade, as President De Brosses has pointed out, can cut off someone's head "like a turnip"; or cleave a gondolier's in two, beneath a bridge. When Corvo fell into the water, he continued to smoke his pipe, just like Byron, who when he floated on his back in the middle of the Grand Canal, kept his cigar in his mouth in order (he said) "not to lose sight of the stars"; his man-servant would follow behind, in a gondola, with his master's clothes on his arm.

Corvo, the author of the famous *Hadrian VII*, which dates from 1904 and which only became successful after the war—while waiting to be revived on stage—has left us a letter about his impressions of Venice that is as beautiful as a page from the *Confessions*: a sleepless night on the Lagoon. Here is Corvo, beneath the stars, accompanied by his two gondoliers, on whose knees he is dreaming: "A twilight world of cloudless sky and smoothest sea, all made of warm, liquid, limpid heliotrope and violet and lavender, with bands of burnished copper set with emeralds, melting, on the other hand, into the fathomless blue of the eyes of the prides of peacocks." Every bit the:

> *Gilding pale streams with heavenly alchemy*

of Shakespeare's thirty-third sonnet.

Chateaubriand wrote that "nobody has penetrated the gondoliers' way of life"; this was something that was reserved for Corvo, as he presents himself to us, taking his revenge on those who barred his way to the priesthood, rejecting honours while at the same time eager for them, and imagining himself seated on a pontifical throne from which he could spit upon the evil World; it is almost as if we can see him, this Corvo, ejected from every inn, his tattered clothes lying in a dirty linen basket at the bottom of his boat, knocking at every door, constantly on the verge of suicide, sitting just above the surface of the water, in the middle of winter, writing, in a huge exercise-book, his *Letters to Millard* which no one would ever be able to read, a Corvo who was the shame of the British community whose charity he had exhausted, who was deprived by the winter of his wealthy English clientele for whom he procured a few of the little beggar boys who, dumbstruck with admiration, used to follow him around, before he set off, the earliest hippy, to the Lido, where he slept on the beach, powerless against attacks from rats and crabs....

1913–1970 LITTLE VENICE

IN LONDON, I only encountered Venice in the district to the north of Paddington station, which was not yet the sought-after area it is today,[18] and which artists had nick-named "Little Venice". At the end of the Edgware Road, the endless four-mile avenue that stretches from Marble Arch to Maida Vale, there is a mournful waterway, the Grand Union Canal, which links the River Thames to Birmingham. Once upon a time, it was countryside; the famous Mrs Siddons died there, far from the stage; Hogarth was married at St Mary's Church, and beneath a tree here, the Brownings became engaged. Regent's Park was extended by Nash who, at the end of the Napoleonic wars, and to the greater glory of George IV, designed this park and those noble neo-classical residences; being a pro-moter of the new canal, he planted it with trees, embell-ishing it with some delightful temples painted in ivory, with black doors and windows; along its quays, they have sur-vived the bombs and the demolition men.

I often used to take a breath of fresh air in Blomfield Road, strolling beneath the hundred-year-old plane trees that sheltered the occasional barge. No one else ventured this far out.

Nowadays,[19] barges, narrow-boats (including the *Jason*, which takes children to and from the Zoo) and sailing boats are moored beneath willow trees swarming with seagulls: you can even see a *Bucintoro* anchored there, with a floating art gallery. Amateur sailors come here in summer, sleeping on board their boats and seeking sustenance in places with names like Ristorante Canaletto or Trattoria Adriatica, where black women supply campers with Chinese take-away dishes; the waters are steeped in silence, the quite breathable air is no longer that of London, and the water-buses that a century and a half ago used to sail up and down the route to Limehouse, on the Thames, no longer pass through the mouldy brick walls of the locks; Little Venice remains one of the last secret corners of London. It helps those who are yearning to escape to the Lagoon to be patient.[20]

1914

A s a frenchman living in England, I continued to dream of myself as a Venetian. In London, Paul Cambon[21] peered at the orange and black curtains of my window at the embassy, which might have been painted by Bakst; "One of my cubist attaché's notions", he sighed.

I have come across a letter written from London, to my mother, shortly before the war, on the 11th of July 1914:

"Yesterday evening we had a terrifically impressive Longhi party, given by a Mrs C. On the terrace, on the rooftop, in the middle of town, a lake had been constructed upon which gondolas floated. This lake was festooned with some marvellous Japanese lanterns that looked like huge luminous oranges; a bizarrely shaped hump-backed bridge, orange-coloured too, crossed over it, a real Rialto from Yokohama, brought back by some Marco Polo or other. The dining-room was Venetian rococo, painted by J.M. Sert, in the same style as his silver and gold designs for the ballet Joseph, which Diaghilev has just put on at Covent Garden. A large table was arranged in a horse-shoe and laid for a hundred people; in front of each guest a silver plate and a candle had been placed: pheasants and peacocks, adorned with feathers, served as display pieces; the table was covered in gold cloth; in the centre of the horse-shoe was a carpet made from the skin of a polar bear, upon which Egyptian dancers and jugglers performed. The servants were dressed in dark tunics with wide white collars. Everybody wore the bauta *over their full-length Longhi coats; masks and three-cornered hats were obligatory. I was dressed in the caftan of a Turk from the Riva degli Schiavoni. Baron de*

Meyer (the foremost photographer of our time) was dressed as Louis XV, in gold lamé, with a silver wig and a bauta *in black* point de Venise. *It was the first time that I had seen a private entertainment done with such bold taste and such sumptuousness in London. As a social gathering, we were on the confines of the real world."*

I had first discovered London in 1902 or 1903; the last of the troops that had been demobilized after the Boer War were gradually returning from South Africa: what a proud conquest of the world it was, by Jingo!

Since my wandering mind has led me to London once more, I shall make a detour, through time and space. London, in any case, was the Venice of the universe at that time. One after another, without interruption, the little omnibuses with their brightly coloured advertisements passed by; you climbed aboard even when it was raining, on double-deckers, your legs covered with horse blankets beneath black wax-cloths. The "cabbies", who drove the cabs, those "London gondolas", as Disraeli called them, sported pink carnations in the button-holes of beige overcoats with mother-of-pearl buttons. I was taught that when accompanying a lady, I should proffer my left hand to assist her on to the cabriolet's high running board, while the right arm should be interposed between her dress and the cab's large wheel to protect her from the mud; the horse flew off, for the cab weighed no more than the prow of a gondola, and you felt as if your protecting hand would never ever touch the ground again. Leicester Square was then the hub of the music halls, those places of perdition to which those under the age of fifteen were forbidden. Pubs, too, were places where ladies were never seen, being frequented only by cleaning women, costermongers, and, once dusk had fallen, the whores. Around Covent Garden, where the fruit and vegetables were piled high, as far as the Opera House, flower-sellers would offer buttonholes of gardenia to gentlemen in tails, as in *Pygmalion*. On the damp pavements, minstrels, smeared in soot, played upon an entirely new instrument, the banjo; you might have imagined yourself to be at the Fondaco dei Turchi, by the Rialto.

I was taken to pantomimes at Drury Lane, London's Châtelet; to the "Chamber of Horrors" at Mme Tussaud's, the English Musée Grévin, or to the Maskelyne Theatre, the Robert-Houdin[22] of the period. It was the age of the great Edwardian actors, of whom there were then a good dozen including Irving, Beerbohm Tree (my father wrote a socialistic play for Tree, that took place in the sulphur mines of Sicily, which Tree never performed), Charles Wyndham and George Alexander. Frank Harris told me about his last visit to Maupassant, at the time that Maupassant was staying with Doctor Blanche, behaving like an animal and walking about on all fours. All these gentlemen wore shiny top-hats and frock coats; in the evening they never wore dinner jackets, but rather tails, and instead of white waistcoats, black ones, together with what were known as "opera hats", which were sold by Gibus, the hat shop, near Trafalgar Square.

In the City, one heard a great deal of German spoken, while much of England's wealth was being made in the East, in South Africa, in the first Russian oil wells, and in

South America, which had been snatched from the Spanish a hundred years earlier and which, just like Venice's wealth which lasted until the time of Christopher Columbus, was an inexhaustible source of riches up until 1914.

It was the era of Kipling's empire, of Wells's science fiction; the figure of Oscar Wilde, wearing a green carnation on the lapel of his grey frock coat, his chest bursting out of his waistcoat, had only recently disappeared from the Burlington Arcade (*Cavendo tutus*); my father had accompanied his funeral procession as far as the Bagneux cemetery. Filling O. W.'s favourite place at the Café Royal, that London version of Florian's, which had originally been a café frequented by French refugees from the Commune, the great Italian singers held sway, presided over by Isidore de Lara: la Tettrazini, la Melba and Caruso. Sherlock Holmes had just made his first appearance with *The Hound of the Baskervilles*, which was serialised in translation in *Le Temps*. Sandow, the strongest man in the world, flaunted his swollen torso on posters in Regent Street and Piccadilly. Railway stations were covered in advertisement hoardings, such as those for *Stephens's Ink*, which, with their great splashes of blue ink, were already heralding abstract painting. Devonshire House, next door to the newly opened Ritz, was still a brick-built castle, in the middle of London. "A Bicycle made for Two" was hummed at Henley regattas. Gilbert and Sullivan's operettas were playing to packed houses at the Savoy: *Iolanthe* or *The Mikado*. Sickert and the artists from the English colony had returned from Dieppe, under the patronage of George Moore or Jacques-Émile Blanche, while Sargent and Laszlo portrayed the great beauties of the Edwardian or Roosevelt age. Loti, Bourget and Maupassant had had open invitations to dine at the Paris homes of Princess Alice of Monaco or Lady Brooke, the Ranee of Sarawak, to whom I had been introduced by my father, for ten years or more; I had mine in London or Ascot for a further eight years , from 1908 to 1916. At table you could see the *maître d'hôtel* standing to attention behind his mistress, attending to her alone, and behind each guest stood a servant in a white wig. The same sights could be seen aboard the yacht *Princesse Alice*, which would sometimes lie at anchor in front of St Mark's, on its way from Madeira or Monaco: the governess dressed in black from head to foot, the first chambermaid wearing a hat and veil, the footman in morning coat, the kitchen-maids in aprons, the maids who served in the drawing-room wearing lace bonnets, the chambermaids in black silk, the laundry-maids attired in white, as in the novels of Mrs Humphrey Ward. At the Savoy Grill or the Carlton, it was the age of "conversationists", of "raconteurs", of "bons viveurs".

After this London detour, let us return to Venice.

1913

VENICE HAD BECOME the most glittering city in Europe, a sort of summer extension of the Ballets Russes; each of them had their origins in the East. Diaghilev allowed himself to be followed around here by his favourites, and his favourites hung around here, ever ready to extricate him from financial situations that were so desperate that at eight o'clock in the evening, he was never sure that he would be able to see the curtain rise at his shows, one hour later. How often have I heard his rich female admirers get up from the table: "Serge is on the phone; there won't be any performance this evening, nobody has been paid." In London, at Cavendish Square, I saw the conductor Beecham, the future Sir Thomas, dashing off to see Sir Joseph, his father, to bring back some money; Emerald got away with a bit of a fright.

La Pavlova opened a ballet school; Grand-Duke Michael entertained on Sundays at Kenwood, Oxford educated the youth of Russia, from Youssoupoff to Obolensky.

1913

I NO LONGER BREATHED the air of Venice except through intermediaries.

That October, I watched the girls I went out with in London returning to England, thrilled to have been able to get close to Nijinsky or Fokine in St Mark's Square; already they were calling them by their first names. They brought back rich spoils, having stripped Venice, that great highway-woman, emptied the Merceria of its last lengths of velvet adorned with golden pomegranates, its green lacquer cabinets, and its glassware. I still think of them as young girls, forgetting that my companions are, or will be, in their eighties: one of them has died from a life of dissipation, too fragile for the alcoholic lures of sur-realism and for handsome Blacks; she was the purest of creatures, the most damaged by life; another, the most beautiful, has experienced everything, the triumphs of stage and society, the thrills of historic moments, the most prominent of embassies; Time seems unable to wear down the marble of this statue…; a third lived a long and spectacular life, before falling into the inkwell, where she is still writing her memoirs; the fourth, the poorest of them, seeing that her youth was coming to an end, spent her last guinea on hiring an evening dress for the night; at the party, she would make the acquaintance of a South African magnate, who married her and made her happy.

1914

In venice, the little French circle I had known in my
youth had become a literary coterie. "Here comes the
Muhlfeld salon", they used to say in St Mark's Square
upon spotting Henri de Régnier. I possess many books of
his that were inscribed to my father, I was mad about his
La Cité des eaux and I lapped up his *Esquisses vénitiennes*,
never expecting that a few years later Henri de Régnier
would submit my first story to the *Mercure de France*. He
stayed at the Palazzo Dario, the home of a Frenchwoman;
behind his proud profile would appear Edmond Jaloux,
Vaudoyer, Charles du Bos, Abel Bonnard, Émile Henriot,
the brothers Julien and Fernand Ochsé, who had trans-
ported their mother's coffin (Cocteau confirmed this) into
their Second Empire dining-room at Neuilly. To me they
all looked alike; you could imagine them dancing a faran-
dole on some hump-backed rialto, made of tarred wood,
such as the one in the *Miracle of the True Cross*, a bridge
linking Paris to Venice, leading them from the Fenice to
the new Théâtre des Champs-Élysées, which had been
opened by Astruc the day before. Excepting myself, I used
to call them the long moustaches; moustaches from
which with the help of a magnifying glass you might have
plucked a few tufts of Vercingétorix's hair, some of
Barbey d'Aurevilly's whiskers, two or three hairs belonging to Flaubert's boys, and last of all, one snatched from
the Lion of St Mark's Square. For these sensitive souls,
Venice was their Mecca. Jaloux brought along his

Henri de Régnier

Marseilles accent, Marsan his cigars, Miomandre his talent as a dancer, Henri Gonse his rough and ready knowledge, and Henri de Régnier his look of a poplar tree that has shed its leaves in autumn; a delightful man, whose sense of humour maintained a close watch over his love life, the curves of his body ran counter to one another in a backwash of counter-curves, rather like the gilt wood or stucco of a piece of Venetian rococo.

They all rallied to the celebrated war-cry of their master Henri de Régnier: "*Vivre avilit* " (Living debases), pursuing a Walpolesque, Byronic or Beckfordian dream; they were like disillusioned Princes de Ligne, austerely gentle, full of witty sayings in the manner of Rivarol,[23] easily bored, quick to anger, chivalrous, and irritated by everything which life had denied them; they would gather at Florian's, in front of a glass-framed painting, "beneath the Chinese one" as they used to say; they collected "bibelots", a word that no longer has any meaning nowadays, lacquer writing cases, engraved mirrors or jasper walking-canes.

They passed around the best addresses among one another: those for *point de Venise* laceware, for chasubles and stoles; Jaloux would spend his literary prize money at these places; the only wealthy one among them, Gonse, bought himself a wardrobe that was supposed to have belonged to Cardinal Dubois; in order not to melt the lacquer, Gonse never lit a fire in his studio on the Plaine Monceau, but sat in his pelisse, blowing on his fingers to keep warm.

The older ones among them dressed in black; only Jean-Louis Vaudoyer dared wear English cloth.

They knew their Venice like the back of their hands:

"I still remember St Mark's Square when it had its campanile," Régnier explained; "do you know that at nine fifty-five, when the building fell down, my gondolier came out with this admirable remark: 'This campanile disintegrated without killing anybody; it collapsed like a man of honour, *è stato galantuomo.*'"

"And what is more honourable still," added Vaudoyer, "is that it collapsed on the 14th of July, as a tribute to the Bastille."

The English have perhaps never loved Florence, nor the Germans Rome, as much as those Frenchmen loved Venice; if Proust dreamed Venice, they lived and relived her, in her glory as well as in her decadence.

"At the Palazzo Grimani…", Gilbert de Voisins, Taglioni's grandson, began.

"Sorry…. Specify your surroundings, my friend; to which Palazzo Grimani do you refer, there are eleven; the one in Santo Polo?"

"Or the one at San Tonia?"

"…Is it the one at Santa Lucca?"

"…Or the one at Santa Maria Formosa?"

"Or do you mean the Palazzo Grimani that's known as 'della Vida'?"

At the time of day when they met for their mysterious *"ponche à l'alkermès"*,[24] the ritual drink that is mentioned on every page of *Heures* or *L'Altana*, these fanatical pilgrims would consult one another, their renowned moustaches yellowing from the smoke of their Virginia cigars. Where would they dine? At which *osteria* (that was the word they used)?

"At the Capello Nero…"

"At the Trovatore…"

"At the Bonvecchiati…"

"At the taverna at the Fenice?"

"At Colombo's, in the Goldoni district?"

"Bottegone's, in Calle Vallaresso?"

They had not been Rimbauds; none of them would ever be a Gide, whom they loathed, nor a Giraudoux, whom they preferred, nor Proust, whom they scarcely knew.[25] Gide, Giraudoux and Proust had also worn their moustaches long; from now on they would shave them off, or trim them.

These were very charming men, who had little self-confidence, they were embittered and sweet-natured dandies, easily amused or driven to despair, who made fun of inverts such as Thomas Mann's hero, that Herr von Aschenbach who was bothered by the naked shoulder that a young man bathing at the Lido had dared to reveal beneath his bathrobe!

Women had brought them pain (they were unlucky, they had had to deal with the last generation of women who would make men suffer). They were proud creatures, refined to a degree, whose nerves were made of Murano spun glass; they were refugees in the City of Refuge, who had been jostled about by life, by a vulgar public, that was not yet well-informed or snobbish, and by publishers who were still tight-fisted; they cared not for riches except at the homes of the Rothschilds, where they dined, but not for the sake of wealth alone.

"You look the spitting image of your father", Vaudoyer

told me, on the day before he died. As I grow older, I feel even closer to them than I did at the age of twenty; without the monocle, that is; their own monocles, already literary appurtenances, would be bequeathed to Tzara, who would arrive shortly from Zurich, and later to Radiguet (his was so big that it pulled out his lower eyelid when it eventually reached it). Nobody wore a monocle with such hauteur, his head thrown back, as did Henri de Régnier; his was a sort of bull's eye hollowed out of the dome of his polished skull, rather like a sixth cupola at St Mark's. Their winter drug was tea; Jaloux, Abel Bonnard and Du Bos served it to the ladies with full Mandarin rites; authors' royalties, had they had any, would have been repugnant to them. They were all more or less poor.

As far as the art of good living was concerned, their time was badly chosen; they might have said, as did Paul Bourget to Corpechot, on the 11th of November 1918: "It is now that disaster begins."

Rather like the campanile that was so dear to Henri de Régnier, at the end of their lives these great lovers of Venice simply collapsed, without a sound, and became "men of honour".

II
THE
QUARANTINE
FLAG

A NIGHT IN VENICE, EARLY 1918

IT WAS NO LONGER a time for engraved mirrors or little Negro boys made from spun glass.

The Palace of the Ancients was in danger of collapse.

After a lightning visit to the borders of the Veneto, where the French general staff was trying to raise Italian morale, I was waiting for a train which didn't arrive. Venice's old railway station was illuminated by the beams of searchlights from the Anglo-French torpedo-boats that patrolled the Adriatic; bright flares fired from sixty Venetian forts had put an end to the Austrians' rather ineffectual raids. What remains with me is the unreality of that autumn night, in which the dome of San Simeone Piccolo—as ever—loomed up, before dipping its head in the Grand Canal once more, while, in turn, San Simeone Grande was lit up, and then the Scalzi bridge and church, that solid, joyful setting out of some ecclesiastical operetta with its display of grandiloquent emblems on its façade (we forget that Bernini was also a playwright).

That night, as a crescent moon vainly awaited its next phase, in a sky that was very dark, I suddenly became aware of a transformation in the war; the wind of defeat was blowing over Rome, where Giolitti's comfortable neutrality was already regretted; only burgeoning fascism swore loyalty to the Entente; its supporters were then no more than a handful of devotees ready to shout: *Vive la France*!

A year spent in Paris had just made me the astonished

81

witness of the fallibility of our leaders. There was the swaggering Viviani ("they are destroyed"), the predictions of Joffre in 1914 ("it will be over by Christmas"), and of Nivelle ("this offensive will be the last"). Day by day the older generations were losing their glamour.

It was not for me to protest because two hundred thousand men had been sacrificed in trying to cross a river, and I was not entitled to speak on behalf of my brothers who were still at war; but being a non-combatant, did I not have a duty to help them, in some other way? Could I not express the mood I was experiencing in a different way? Perhaps, in this gloomy station, in this darkened Venice, my *Nuits* would be conceived? It would be my way of indicating that portents were appearing in the sky. My *Nuits* would speak not in the name of those who had died, but on behalf of the dead, to divert them, to show sympathy for them, to tell them that I never stopped thinking of them, and especially of those classmates of the years 1908–1913 who had been so effectively decimated.

"That shameful period from 1914 to 1918", Larbaud dared to write at that time, in his Alicante *Journal*, speaking as a humanist and as an outraged European, seemed to us, in 1917, like a vague sort of liberation.

"1917, the year of confusion", Poincaré would say later; for us, it was a disturbing year. A year of despair for the only truly cosmopolitan generation that had appeared in France since the Encyclopédistes.

Fourteen months spent on the fringes of power had taught me a great deal;[1] I had seen some great Frenchmen, all of whom hoped for victory, grow suspicious of one another, tear each other apart and exclude one another in the name of the sacred union: Briand, who while approving Prince Sixte's dialogues with Vienna, secretly pursued a policy of pacifism that was condemned severely by the Government; Ribot, who succeeded him, reckoned him to be suspect; and then this same Ribot was soon hounded out by Clemenceau who did not hesitate to let Briand go to the High Court; I admired Philippe Berthelot, who, single-handed, had been responsible for our foreign policy ever since the outbreak of war, refusing to set foot in the Élysée, where Poincaré awaited him in vain for four years and never forgave him for this insult. I had observed the unjust, but total disgrace of Berthelot, who was sacrificed by Ribot to a Parliament he openly despised, a Berthelot who was abruptly forgotten by all of those who had previously hung about at his heels, soliciting diplomatic assignments or extensions, until Clemenceau, having noticed how this great servant of the State had been slandered, took him back into his service. This same "Tiger" Clemenceau admitted to a weakness for Joseph Caillaux; he would have been sorry to have had him shot. I remember what Jules Cambon, at the end of his life, told me about Clemenceau: "Against my wishes, Clemenceau made me one of the five delegates to the Versailles Conference. The Anglo-Saxon delegates who were there worked together. For our part, we never had any meetings … I was never given any instructions at all. André Tardieu was the only one among us who had any idea what Clemenceau was thinking.... The Tiger was still like some elderly student, fairly ignorant, not very intelligent, but generous and tenacious.... As far as war is concerned, one has to admire his ability, for he succeeded, but what a pity that he took it upon himself to make peace!"

The treachery of office life, the effeteness of the salon, the treachery of the parliamentary corridor, the semi-blackmail that went on, the sound of the safe's combination lock being opened for secret funds or for journalists' "envelopes": the whole complexity of political machinery had been paraded before the young and insignificant attaché I was in 1916 and 1917.

At that moment, on the eve of my departure for Rome, as 1917 gave way to 1918, I jotted down in the last pages of my *Journal*, the impression that the war suddenly made on me: "It has a different stench, it's a Luciferean conspiracy." Europe was beginning to smell.

From the heart of Italy, life in Paris, where I had just come from, took on another aspect: I had witnessed the terrible year of 1917, when Europe, as we now realize, had almost collapsed; 1917 was the year of peace initiatives, of the Coeuvres and Missu rebellions, when General Bulot had been stripped of his general's stars,[2] of secret battles between the Sûreté Générale [the French criminal investigation department] and the Service des Renseignements aux Armées [the Army intelligence service], and the newspaper *L'Action Française*, which had clashed with *Le Bonnet rouge* and *Le Carnet de la semaine*; the Daudet family offered a curious spectacle: at Mme Alphonse Daudet's home, Georges Auric[3] and I would listen to Léon Daudet preparing for Clemenceau to be given a triumphant welcome to Parliament, while his younger brother Lucien, a supporter of Aristide Briand, and dressed in the uniform of one of Étienne de Beaumont's ambulance crews, yearned for a negotiated peace; every day in *L'Action Française*, Léon Daudet, who, like Philippe Berthelot, had been raised at Renan's knee, called for the indictment of this sort of brother whom he clasped in his arms whenever he met him. (Proust observes this "split personality" in *Contre Sainte-Beuve*.)

Who will write the novel of 1917? Among historians, it is the geometrical turn of mind that simplifies and falsifies everything; only in works of the imagination can the truth be found.

Feverishly, Paris awaited the American troops. Would *they* arrive in time? In pacifist and *zimmerwaldien* Zurich, Tristan Tzara opened the dictionary at random and happened upon the word *dada*. When *Les Mamelles de Tirésias* was performed, Montparnasse had heard Arthur Cravan, a precursor of the anti-establishment, summon "the deserters of seventeen nations", while to the sound of an orchestra of nuts and bolts shaken in an iron box, André Breton, with his hint of a beard, yelled out: "Take to the roads!"

Henceforth, nothing was straightforward: the immobilization of the front lines, the increasingly obscure aims and origins of the war, the Russian revolution which changed people's political stances; in short, everything that the young of 1970 discovered as they watched a film like *Oh, What a Lovely War* we had experienced already.

A golden age had ended; another was emerging, fringed in black.

For three years, my civilian's clothes had weighed heavily on my conscience; the appalling suffering of those who fought had become intolerable to me; all of a sudden to be in Italy was to begin to live again, and this was true not just for me, but for the French troops who landed there and were able to forget the nightmare of trench warfare; it was a surprise to be thinking like Maréchal Brissac who, at the time of the Fronde, charged at a hearse, sword in hand, crying out: "That's the enemy!" From now on, the one enemy was Death: the submerged forces of life surged up into our consciousness; we were no longer in control. The animal wanted to live and its animal nature carried all before it.

"I found Venice in a state of mourning" (*Byron*). Above St Mark's the pigeons had been replaced by the *Tauben* (Austrian aircraft, known as pigeons).

In Venice, through the shattered dome of Santa Maria, one could see the blue sky; the Arsenal was damaged, the walls of the Doges' Palace were cracked, St Mark's was choking beneath fifteen feet of sandbags held in place by beams and wire netting; the horses of the Quadriga had vanished! The Titians had been wrapped up; the canals had been emptied of gondolas, the pigeons had been eaten.

These were the last days of the retreat to the Tagliamento; five hundred kilometres of front-line between Lake Garda and the Adriatic. Mestre was a military zone. In Brescia, in Verona and in Venice the French divisions (like the Germans, in 1943) were doing their best to infuse new courage into the Italians. On the quaysides, French officers were sampling long Virginia cigarettes that were perforated with straws; in the Red Cross lorries, wounded Senegalese soldiers sitting side by side with Neapolitans in their hospital gowns mingled with *bersaglieri*, shorn of most of their feathers, with Austrian prisoners of war, Tyroleans wearing grey-blue uniforms, and with *carabinieri* who had exchanged their cocked hats for a helmet rather like Colleone's; Russian prisoners who had been returned by the Austrians were sweeping the docks with brooms made from leaves of maize; on walls, menacing posters ordered deserters from the Caporetto to rejoin the 4th Corps or risk being "shot in the back".

Rome, upon my return there, resembled the France of 1940, a medieval city ravaged by a moral plague; muddy boots, drenched uniforms, bandaged heads that had been gashed by flints thrown up by exploding shells in the Alps; nobody was working, nobody was where they should be. Rome, as far as I was concerned consisted of the chancellery, among whose green files I roamed, just as in dreams one strolls into a ball wearing one's underpants … I have come across one of my letters to my mother, from the Palazzo Farnese, dated 31 December 1917: "Rome is teeming with refugees from Venice; yesterday I met G. who had left her palazzo on the Grand Canal, carrying her Giorgione in a hat box. St Anthony of Padua was taken to Bologna for safe keeping; the Colleone is here."

Every day at lunch, at Barrère's house, I listened to Foch and Weygand relating how that very morning they had explained to the Italian ministers that the Isonzo front was not the only stage of war and that the two hundred thousand prisoners and two hundred thousand captured Italian guns was not really very dreadful; was not Gabriele D'Annunzio dropping bombs on Trieste and Cattaro?

I was very lonely at the Palazzo Farnese. Before I had left, Proust, discussing Barrère, my future boss, had said to me: "He was a friend of my father's; an old fool…". In my mind I was still living in Paris, where Proust scarcely ever left his bed; Hélène had had an operation; Giraudoux was at Harvard; Alexis Léger[4] in Peking; in the Champagne, Erik Labonne, an artillery officer, was aiming his guns at the Russian troops that had come to France as allies and who were now regarded as suspect; in London, Antoine and Emmanuel Bibesco confessed that they wanted a peace to be negotiated with all speed; "That would ruin things for everybody", predicted Georges Boris, who astonished us with the audacity of his advanced views. At the Palazzo Farnese, I had come across a former colleague from before the war in London, François Charles-Roux, now a secretary at the embassy; our problems had made him more combative and intransigent than ever; it was as if he alone knew how to put the Italians back on a war footing; he thought me apathetic; our friendship was affected as a result; furthermore, the Caillaux affair had introduced a coolness between us.

Joseph Caillaux always amazed me, ever since my first visit to his home in rue Alphonse-de-Neuville in 1911, up until the last one, in 1926; his sudden rages, which made his polished skull turn pink, then crimson, his fiery gaze that was circumscribed by the diamond-studded ring of his monocle, his insolence and his haughty foolhardiness used to fascinate me; my father, whom Caillaux liked, admired him and defended him, as he did at his trial, even if that meant falling out with Calmette's friends. The war had caused Caillaux to lose what little mental stability he had left. Those that succeeded him were glad to be rid of him and had showered him with missions to foreign countries; as he took stock of the world he forgot about all other considerations; the preposterous remarks he made in Argentina, the bad company he kept in Italy, his hopes of negotiating an unconditional peace, his childish gaffes and his daring opinions, the entire make up of his character astonished me, including the way he mixed with comical rogues to whom he willingly entrusted his riches, "not that he particularly liked villains, but they served his particular policies", as Poincaré said of him. Reconciling France and Germany in 1911 would have avoided the suicide of the white race; I had heard Caillaux say that "evicting the southern Europeans from our colonies in North Africa was madness"; he added: "The Arabs will throw us out if we do not henceforth open up Tunisia to the Italians and Orania to the Spanish; with them twenty million Europeans can stand shoulder to shoulder; alas! the blinkered attitude of your Quai d'Orsay is irreversible." Time has passed; I think of Caillaux once more when I reread Clemenceau's bitter reflections on his past life, when he addressed the Senate in October 1919: "The Germans are a great nation; we have to reach an understanding with them; for my part, I have hated them too much; this task is for others, those younger men

who succeed me, to accomplish." Is it not just as if Caillaux
were speaking?

I have always been attracted to lost causes: Fouquet,
Caillaux, Berthelot, Laval. When they were sent to prison,
dragged before the High Court, ignominiously removed
from their duties or sent to the gallows, my affection for
them grew all the more. What was it that linked such varied destinies? Would a psychoanalyst be able to explain
this? It goes back a long way; when asked "Why are you
a Dreyfusard?", I had answered, aged eight, that it was
because there were no others in my class, a reply that was
to remain famous among members of my family, who
actually saw it not so much as an indication of force of
character, but rather of naïvety.

Success followed by failure would remain the theme of
the books I wrote between 1950 and the sixties; after
*Fouquet, Le Flagellant de Séville, Les Clés du souterrain, Le
Dernier Jour de l'Inquisition, Hécate….* As a child, I slept with
my thumbs pressed inside the palms of my hands; psy-
choanalysts saw this as a sign of introversion. Since 1917,
one of my future wife's brothers had lived in Zurich,
where he was treated by Schmit Guisan, a pupil of Freud's
and Jung's; this was how I knew of the existence of psychoanalysis five or six months before this attempt at liberation was known about in France; the contrast between
the hidden sexual life and social life has always filled me
with wonder. Gide says somewhere that he hovered
around psychoanalysis; in my case, it was psychoanalysis
that hovered around me, resoling my former Christian
shoes along the path of penitence.

Those forms of peace that are enforced or negotiated, that are glorious or shameful, are to do with politics; for the writer as for the ploughman, there is only one form of peace, not several. I have only ever loved peace; though this fidelity has brought me some strangely disloyal strokes of luck; it has taken me from a very advanced left-wing position in 1917 to deposit me in 1940 in a Vichy upheld by the ideas of Charles Maurras, where I was no less ill at ease. It is not man himself who changes, it is the world that revolves around him; I have known England in Victorian times, when to use the word "trousers" was frowned upon, only to discover today nowadays an Albion that bathes naked in the fountains of Trafalgar Square; I have seen Russian officers in 1917 with their epaulettes ripped off, only to find a USSR that is concocting thousands of honorary distinctions and reinstating a Mandarin form of hierarchy.

In between the two is that hemiplegic body that we nowadays call Europe....

The reason why these period portraits do not deserve to age too quickly is because, fifty years earlier, they prefigure our present times. In them I can identify that bitterness of someone like Scott Fitzgerald, writing in 1925: "Our parents have done enough of this damage; the old generation practically laid waste to the world before passing it on to us." After 1917, I disassociated myself from my elders, without ever ceasing to accept their bequest; the heartbreak of the emancipated.

In 1917, Marcel Sembat, one of the leaders of the SFIO [the French Socialist party between 1905 and

1971] and a highly cultivated man, befriended me (the ground floor of the Berthelots' home, on the boulevard Montparnasse, adjoined Léon Blum's flat: domestic and foreign policy mingled there, in an atmosphere I associate with the last days of Symbolism, the former *Revue blanche*, Lugné-Poe and Claudel, and which did not survive after 1918). Sembat introduced me to the paintings that were being done by the new generation; I dared to contravene my father's maxim: "As far as Cézanne, but no further"; Sembat, a gentle and tolerant man, humanised socialism; it was due to him that I came to understand that we had to overcome our dread of the working man, one of the legacies of 1848 and 1871.

That year, I met another Socialist leader, Bracke-Desrousseaux; it was at V.M.'s[5] home (during supper, Claudel handed out hard-boiled eggs, on which he had written poems, to each of us). "I believe in socialism, but I can only think of it as national", I remarked innocently to Bracke-Desrousseaux. (I little imagined that, twenty years later, these two words would cause Europe to explode.) He replied dryly: "Impossible; socialism is international in its essence."

1919

AFTER TWO YEARS in Rome and Madrid, I returned to Paris bringing with me some poems that were those of an impatient young man; some were written in Venice, among them this:

Oh! Nous ne pouvons attendre davantage...

(Oh! We can't wait any longer...)

or:

...Nous nous lançons sur la mer sans routes...

(...We embark upon uncharted seas...)

or:

...Nos cadets, on lit dans leurs yeux
Qu'ils ne souffriront pas d'attendre...
...A quand un large et continuel don
de tout à tous?
A quand une grande course, pieds nus, autour
du globe?

(You can see in the eyes of our younger brothers/ that they will not put up with waiting.../ ...When shall we all make generous, continuous sacrifices to one another?/ When shall we race barefooted around the globe?)

A more distant note was struck there; it came from:

...Le Passé ... avec ses
héros, histoire, expérience, en toi engrangés!
L'héritage total qui a convergé vers toi ...

(...The Past ...with its heroes, history and experiences that are stored within you!/ Our entire inheritance which has converged on you...)

The note struck is that of *Leaves of Grass*. For many years the athletic, lush and elemental verse of Walt Whitman had made him my superman. Hugo? By the time I left the *lycée* I had got no further than *Eviradnus* (I would not discover his *Bouche d'ombre* until half a century later). It was in Whitman that I first inhaled the scents of the open road and of woman.

I had thought the itinerant American was unknown in France; I was wrong; translated in 1907, the lessons he preached had not been lost; I encountered them in unanimism and in the work of Duhamel and Romains; Whitman had inspired Cendrars's *Pâques à New York*; following in his footsteps, Cocteau had just sailed down the Potomac; Whitman was assumed to be the inspiration for Supervielle's *Débarcadères* and *Gravitations*, just as he had fascinated Barnabooth, the tramp dressed by Henry Poole: in the United States, Hemingway and Dos Passos had taken high altitude rest cures with Whitman.

I am for those who march abreast
with the whole world ...

It was the last echo of an international romanticism, of the year 1848 stretched out on a planetary scale.

1920

Opening of harry's bar (before Orson Welles and Hemingway).

1922 OUVERT LA NUIT[6]

AFTER THE WAR of 1870, those attending Flaubert's *cénacle*—his literary gatherings—were searching for an overall title for what was to become *Les Soirées de Médan*, made famous by *Boule-de-Suif*, and apparently almost called the anthology: *La Guerre comique*; this casual reaction was not blasphemy, but rather a sigh in the wake of great danger; the same could be observed in 1918; this explains, and may perhaps excuse, my *Nuits*.

In the colourful language they used at the time, the critics were very easy-going about the superficiality of a book that cocked a snook at the vast wide world, the world of fifty years ago that still seemed immense. It was a cry of happiness at having survived, one that struck a false note in an age that was already impoverished; a happiness for which friends of mine, such as Proust or Larbaud, who were very ill, envied me; all I longed for was a little of their genius, whereas they used to say: "I should have liked to live like Morand." (Without knowing each other, each of them said exactly that.) May they not envy me for the time I spent "living well". How much time was lost in making up time! Larbaud, responding to my *De la vitesse* ["On speed"], dedicated his essay *La Lenteur* ["Slowness"] to me; he was the true voluptuary.

1921

A NOTHER HALT at this Venice railway station "which terminates at nothing, upon a large tank of shadow and silence" (*Ouvert la nuit*); thus begins *"La Nuit turque"*, which I completed yesterday.

That day, I continued my journey as far as Stamboul, travelling on a brand new Simplon-Express, the train with which the Allies intended to depose the old Orient-Express, planned by Wilhelm II as the first section of his *"Bagdadbahn"*.

On terra firma, the trenches were being filled in, the children of Venice were fishing in the shell craters, and frogmen from the Arsenal were helping re-float the Austrian torpedo boats that had sunk or become silted up.

It was a Venice still drowsy after its wartime slumber....

In *La Fausse Maîtresse*, Balzac had written: "The carnival in Venice is no longer worthwhile; the real carnival is happening in Paris."

That was true, too, of the 1920s.

It is not my intention to describe the Paris of those days; my purpose here is merely a tête-à-tête with Venice, the tempo of these pages being that of the ebb and flow of life on her shores.

Everything that took place in Paris during my years of absence confirmed the changes in social behaviour that had begun in 1917. A generation of people had returned from the war, disenchanted by the past and curious about the future, and about those who tried to explain it and unveiled the new world to them, providing them with a geographical assessment of their unexplored dwelling place, our planet. If my *Nuits* and *Rien que la Terre* were well received at the time, it was due to circumstances rather more than to the author: success is frequently nothing more than a man's confrontation with the age in which he lives.

What is art, if it is not that which constitutes each age?

Quite unconsciously each one of our books seemed to be saying to everything that happened before the war: "This will help to bury you." In every age, the fallow deer have moaned about the ten-pointer stags; all of a sudden, we were experiencing that miracle, repeated regularly since 1798, of not having anyone in front of us; our fathers and grandfathers had decamped and were fading into memory; everything was empty, wide open and available. We never knew that long period of youthful revolt, that stretches from the Romantics to the post-1968 Leftists: "Advance or perish."

It was a kind of instant, total freedom, a path that chance had unblocked and which one then discovers is—in every domain—bare, just as much in the art of Picasso and the dance of Massine, as in the parties thrown by Étienne de Beaumont (in his town house in the rue Masséran, situated, ironically, between the noble faubourg and Montparnasse)—parties that were described by Raymond Radiguet and that put the Persian balls of the pre-1914 era firmly back into the Musée Grévin. The public threw itself into the avant-garde with such passion that not only was there no rear-guard, but there were no troops either.

How did I come to find myself hurled from among the

front ranks of the Ancients, how had a youth spent among the anchorites fitted me for the avant-garde? I still wonder. Was it the surge of the new generation carrying me along in its wake? Our publishers' hysterical greed for publicity was never more than a turbo engine that exploited the force of a tide that launched talents as different as Montherlant or Breton into prominence.

What a stampede! Every snob wanted to be a part of it, to experience this new adventure and to belong to the perimeter of this literary Kamchatka of which Baudelaire speaks. The old generation asked for mercy and praised us to the skies, offering us reviews, honours, friendship and the hands of their daughters at comical lunch parties at which we were flanked at table by academicians who promised us the moon; most of them loathed us, just as people have always loathed those who come after them. "What should we think of you, Maître?" asked the members of Les Six of their senior, Maurice Ravel, who wittily replied: "Loathe me." (They did nothing of the sort, incidentally; their loathing stopped with Wagner.)

For those of the pre-1914 era, we were insurgents, hungry for blood, members of a new sect of Carnivores who were derisively turning the Establishment upside down, forerunners of those "Barbarians" whose coming Barrès had long predicted; we took over Marinetti's restaurant, howling at the death of Venice and making fun of the gondolas, "those idiot's see-saws"; along the Champs-Élysées, Max Jacob and Cocteau called out to the children: "Hurry up and play, little casualties of the next war!" Literature's old guard protested about this Proust

Jean Cocteau, 1934

"whose budding groves prevailed over the groves of the sacrificial heroes"; the "Wooden Crosses"[7] denounced *Le Diable au corps* in which the *poilus* are cuckolds.

Today those "*années folles*" shock us because of the number of victims they bequeathed us—the suicides, the hopeless, the deserters, the failures. How many Picassos may have been left behind! "I have cut through tradition like a good swimmer crossing a river"; what Picasso did not add was that Hans, the flute player, was followed when he swam by rats who, in their case, drowned.

Jean Cocteau, who had moved on from his Venetian poems of 1909, took risks which for anyone else would have been perilous; he always landed on his feet again. More acclaimed than ever, having acquired a new public and created a second youth for himself, he was everywhere at once; he couldn't miss the bus because he ran in front of it; he was at the forefront of everything, the spiciest of metaphors on the nib of his pen, and because of his sarcastic turn of phrase he adopted a high-pitched voice; with his questioning chin, his gimlet-like expression and his fingers weaving in and out, he lived his life "at full tilt". To have taken a rest would have blunted his talents. Electric sparks hissed from Cocteau-le-Pointu from all sides. Going down the Henri III staircase after visiting him in the block of flats in the rue d'Anjou where his mother lived, you felt foolish, retarded, stiff-jointed and slow-witted; only he was able to sleep as he danced, on the tips of his toes.

At the other extreme, confident of their genius and determined to flee from *le Tout-Paris* and its poison, Saint-John

Perse (at that time known as Saint-Léger Léger), who was back from China, and Giraudoux held firm, deaf to all else but the very personal tones of *Éloges* (1911) and *Provinciales* (1908).

But the bell had tolled for them too; in their own way they would be induced to live in and occupy "the positions that had been relinquished", as the recent official communiqués used to put it.

Here is an example: Round about the mid-1920s. A dinner-party at the home of Erik Labonne, in the flat in which he still lives in avenue Victor-Emmanuel; four young men on the staff of the Foreign Office, who had become friends while taking the competitive entrance examinations (even though they had sat their exams on different dates): Giraudoux, who was forty-four years old, Alexis Léger (Saint-John Perse), Erik Labonne and I, who were all thirty-five. Philippe Berthelot, our director, our boss and our friend, had just experienced one of those terrifying reversals of fortune which destroyed the end of his life; from now on it would be a matter of consolidating our administrative positions without him, and of maintaining continuity; let no one imagine us as over-excited young men eager to be in command; we had been through the war and had learnt how to control ourselves; we were simply obeying a "duty to be ambitious" (*Stendhal*). All of a sudden, we had become orphans; the great generation of French diplomacy—the Cambon brothers, Paléologue, Jusserand—had recently disappeared; between it and ourselves, there were only civil servants.

This is how fate would deal with us in that period when

everything seemed to be in limbo and the future was abruptly turning into the present:

With the death of Berthelot, Alexis Léger, who was in the Far Eastern department, would gain direct access to his minister Briand, who was Président de Conseil; Briand was one of those intelligent but lazy men who knew how to make use of other people; Alexis Léger convinced his boss and even Parliament that Berthelot had alienated himself: for over ten years, serving under many ministers, he was to remain the master of French diplomacy; Erik Labonne, however, was a mystic: he had foreseen—almost through revelation, or inspiration, that our colonies in North Africa were overflowing with hidden oil; to begin with, nobody listened to him; with great tenacity he devoted his life to substantiating his beliefs: the results are well known. Here too, it was a case of *tabula rasa*. As for Giraudoux, he pursued two dreams: to serve in the government of his country, an illusion that was not so much incompatible with his genius, as with his character; it was fifteen years later that Daladier gave him his opportunity, at the Continental, in 1940; his other dream was the theatre: for a quarter of a century—ever since Maeterlinck or Claudel—there had been nobody; when his play *Siegfried* was acclaimed two years later, French theatres were empty.

And so what was the target of my own aspirations? For my friends, it was their work, their career, or both. All I dreamed of was complete freedom; and yet from a very young age I had been left unsupervised and been given a choice of careers; I had never felt I was being held back at the office, or if I was, only very gently so. So what did I think that total liberation or the sort of independence which only death can supply would give me? I still ask myself this question. Was it the sort of life of a "hippie", before the term was invented, a journey towards some non-existent happiness, an abandonment to a lethargy which had more to do with illness than with good health? I search my memory trying to recall my state of mind at the time: being on this earth is a unique adventure; I had to make the most of it. To do what? To raise oneself up to man's estate or satisfy one's instincts? All of this, and simultaneously. Don't think about it; forward march, head down! God will look after his own; let's see what happens.

Two guardian angels, my mother and my wife, having a deep sense of tradition as well as being aware of my best interests, decided differently. A life was something you constructed like a house, according to their way of thinking.

All I longed for was independence, not knowing that it is in short supply. Everything, straight away! Unaware that we pay for being "quick". How unfair to make us wait! I wanted the whole world, one without end (did I carry within me the seeds of that mania for evasion in which people delight today?) Recognizing that I was not very adept at controlling others and at getting what I wanted, I sought to shape my life as if it were some precious substance, to hew away all rough edges and restore it to all its prismatic power.

Everything was available, everything was waiting to be plucked; everything was; the larger obstacles would await us twenty years later. Another story.... The time has not come to tell it.

Those who try to recreate that period of fifty years ago imagine it as some immense Bal des Quat'Zarts, parading before an astonished and uncomprehending Paris; that is to miss the point entirely. We were artists delighted at the acceptance we were given by an increasingly well-informed public. We were living through a veritable springtime of work, research, new inventions and of friendship between the arts; rather like the Impasse du Doyenné at the time of Nerval. Everything moved forward along the same axis, open to the road ahead, in an atmosphere of reciprocity, generosity and true cama-raderie. The Muses fraternised; those who had previously been forgotten we restored to their true position: Georges Auric, at the age of fifteen, thought the world of Léon Bloy and used to visit him, Poulenc rescued Satie from the depths of Arcueil, and we brought back Valéry from out of the shadows; the theatre alone continued to snore away on the boulevard. Artists created backdrops for the stage, and Derain painted sets for Massine; Darius Milhaud and I spent the summer of 1920 together in Juan-les-Pins's only hotel, a small boarding-house for travelling salesmen called the Hôtel de la Gare; Radiguet, in order not to have to return home to the suburbs, would spend the night among Brancusi's blocks of polished metal; Reverdy wrote his poems in the rue Cambon, while another great artist was busy fitting her clients.

Romanticism had survived for so long that its last vestiges still existed half a century later; it constructed no more lasting temples to its gods, however, than the present age does to its idols of the 1920s; 1970 is still illuminated by the lamps they lit; from Picasso to Kisling, from Proust to Saint-John Perse, from Honegger to Satie, the masters of those days have never had their authority questioned; and Gabrielle Chanel, who dressed the Deauville of 1915 in her jerseys, was still dressing high society of the 1970s in her outfits. They represented the true portfolio of stocks and shares of their day, the real Suez, the real I.B.M. It is a phenomenon that has to do with the athletic qualities of the artists of the heroic age. The boulder has continued to gather pace, and a great number of trees have been felled: yet not one of the geniuses of the 1920s has been dislodged.

It's a French phenomenon; you only have to transport yourself mentally to the Berlin of the expressionists, the England of Huxley, the Rome of Malaparte, or the New York of the *Dial* to compare how fortunate Paris was at that time. The other day (1970) I was in New York, in the same Algonquin bar where in about 1925 we used to meet Mencken, George Nathan, the Ernest Boyds, Carl Van Vechten, Walter Wanger and Scott Fitzgerald; seeing nothing but ghosts in the famous "roaring twenties" grill room and dining-room, I observed that whereas the force of the storm and the lust for life had toppled our American friends off their perches, we had been more fortunate or more wise, in this Paris in which Dos Passos used to relate how, after wild nights out, I used to protect him, Cummings and Gilbert Seldes from being beaten up.[8]

106

I can see myself opening an envelope from the N.R.F.: it's my first cheque from Gallimard; I felt pleased, yet at the same time irritated; I had never been paid any salary except by the State; I had the feeling that I was betraying it, not freeing myself from it. Many civil servants, from Maupassant to Valéry, have lived in this way, one that was honourable and accepted by everyone, but they had not belonged to the "*grand corps*",[9] the War Office, the Admiralty, the Treasury, the Audit Office, the Department of Transport, the Conseil d'État, the Foreign Office, etc...the schools which trained you for these professions constituted bodies in whose eyes the State was sacrosanct; and the entrance examinations for them (the "Concours") were a sort of gateway to the top. What did an entrance examination consist of, particularly in those days? A formality, in which one's popularity rating and a sort of common law were what chiefly mattered; nevertheless, a man who wasn't "a product of the Concours", and who had entered these top careers through prefectural channels, through journalism or by political means, was never quite considered as an equal. State salaries were not generous, but this money was something special; it was not other people's money; nobody had ever touched it; the six louis d'ors granted me each month for ten years were, at least until 1918, newly minted by the Banque de France.

This cult of the State still exists today, but people nowadays often become employed in the civil service as if for a training period, they branch out into the Banque de France (the slang term is *pantouflage*[10]), private interests come into play and the boundary lines separating a diplomatic ambassadress from an ambassadress of fashion have become blurred; the numerous international organisations, the way in which one's colleagues are selected, the infiltration of large companies through side entrances, by publicity methods, by press or cultural attachés, all these must have altered the attitudes of the staff in the civil service, such as I knew it.

Parisian life and my stormy experiences among the varied milieux of the capital would gradually dampen the respect I felt for that unwritten code of honour and loosen the bonds that bound me morally just as tightly as the diplomatic corps had coerced an officer in the time of Alfred de Vigny. Seeing my name suddenly in bookshop windows felt like setting foot in another country; it was the end of that absolute anonymity that for so long had been the Civil Service's golden rule. When I returned to the "office", my former kingdom, on the eve of the last war, I did not find what I had relinquished twelve years previously; politics, the post-1936 trade union mentality, the new intellectual approach, the arrival of École Normale graduates in the profession, meant that it no longer had quite the same atmosphere; I sometimes came across the last vestiges of former days tucked away in the hotel rooms of Vichy.

I feel sure that there are just as many great civil servants as there were, perhaps more, for the country has grown smaller; they will probably get used to life within the hexagon that is France.

I can only think of a hexagon as something etched in the spheres.

1925

A LOVE OF THE ROAD

A PHOTOGRAPH that is often reproduced shows the composers known as Les Six,[11] Valentine Hugo and myself in one of those fairground boats painted on canvas; I am leaning over the rails, throwing up, and Valentine is supporting my head; it is the very image of the way I felt in 1925; the post-war years gave me a sudden desire to be sick.

In Paris I was becoming the "cosmopolitan Parisian", as sketched in crayon by Vlaminck in his *Portraits avant décès*. The "Bœuf" in the rue Duphot had moved to a smart area, and our youth there was over. We left behind us newly published books, black velvet sofas, blue antimacassars, zebra rugs, Russian cabarets, fish-net stockings worn by sirens, claw-like and silver-painted nails, syncopated music, plucked eyebrows, everything to do with the Paris of Van Dongen that the artist was in the process of parading through the provinces, where it was being lapped up. Paris was the city of false life which simultaneously could throw a Katherine Mansfield into Gurdjieff's magnetic snare; people were fleeing towards every outlet, every religion, there were false conversions, instant tonsures, it was the very opposite of Heaven, call-up time for the guardian angels. Paris lost her moral control of the world; she has never regained it again. The "Coupole" in Montparnasse was no longer the universe. Salvation lay in flight! Henceforth, complimentary copies of books would be inscribed: "*On behalf of the author, who is*

The Groupe des Six (from left to right): François Poulenc, Germaine Tailleferre, Louis Durey, Jean Cocteau, Darius Milhaud, Arthur Honegger and a drawing of Georges Auric by Cocteau, 1931

away from Paris." From then on "travelling became my only concern".

In Bangkok, I rediscovered Venice; was it the water or the mainland? "Stretches of land that are so low that they seem to have escaped the sea as if by a miracle", wrote the Abbé de Choisy; in those days Thailand still wore her tiara and called herself Siam. There were the same golden fishing boats, with fifty oarsmen, as on the Lagoon in the time of Guardi; the floating teak rafts and the sampans laden to the brim with paddy rice reminded me of the baskets of fruit along the meandering Brenta; the cabins in which the Siamese stored their dried palms resembled the huts built by the first Veneti, the stupas of the royal Wat Phra Kaew were just like Venice in the time of Marco Polo, and the sailing boats with their unfurled sails that looked like vampires" wings bore the same eye painted on their prows as those of the fishermen in Malamocco.

1926

PHILIPPE BERTHELOT's fall from grace gave me cause for reflection; the complete athlete, he had wanted to experience life to the full, serving the State under Poincaré, playing tennis with Giraudoux, frequenting the Paris of horse racing and dress rehearsals, the Opéra and Lugné-Poe's plays; a man with the administrative orderliness and the intellectual anarchy of a Sturel, who both kept dangerous company and mixed in society,[12] and who set off on journeys lasting two years; he was the author of a sonnet the lines of which rhymed with the syllable *omphe*; he knew the whole of Hugo by heart as well as the stud-book of the Jockey Club from the date of its foundation; he wore himself out both physically (he never slept) and mentally (despising everyone except his colleagues and friends). I realised that you could not serve the State as well as have other masters. There could be no second career. The State demands total dedication. I had to make a choice: I opted for happiness, for the open road, for lost time, that is to say time gained. I set off once more on the road to Venice.

Venice is but the thread of a discourse interrupted by lengthy silences in which, from time to time, different countries have occupied her, just as they have occupied me: twenty-five years in Switzerland, ten years in Tangiers or Spain, eight years in England; not to mention Paris.

Barrès wrote: "This image of my own being and this image of Venice's being tally in a number of ways." My credentials for expressing this are less imposing, but the time I have devoted to Venice may permit me to apply this remark to myself. It is mainly through my past that Venice, as well as Paris, continue to hover without sinking.

LA BRENTA, 1925–1970

HOW MANY TIMES, before the last world war, did I take the little road along the banks of the Brenta to return to Venice from the thermal baths at Abano, near Padua! The tedium of mud baths, which were over by nine o'clock in the morning, drove me away from the *Orologio*, where I had a room in which to spend the night, to Venice, where a room in which I could spend the day awaited me. At that time there was very little traffic between Venice and the mainland; today Padua has become an annexe of Venice, extending it as far as Verona and Vicenza; buses, coaches and lorries run every half-hour between the Eremitani and Piazzale Roma, swallowing up the Lagoon faster than any train; the sleepy, provincial town of Padua is now an important business centre, full of bustle and noise and the sound of gas explosions, and drowning in carbon monoxide fumes that mingle with the foul stench of the Mestre oil refineries, reminiscent of Maracaibo or Sainte-Adresse.

To avoid the *autostrada*, you can travel by water; the Brenta opens its five or six locks to the *Burchiello*, or passenger barge; leaving St Mark's Square the river bank is approached from the west, from Fusina, thus avoiding Mestre and Porto Marghera, which are shrouded in a blackish haze. The *Burchiello* was once the only means of transport, that of Montaigne, of President De Brosses, of Goethe, and of Casanova, whose *Memoirs* open with such a pretty description of this type of horse-pulled barge, of which the Correr Museum possesses a model of the period; it's a boat with painted panels, with mirrors and candles on the walls; travellers wearing masks would gossip away at the bows while the boatmen steered from the back; on the roof is a an area surrounded by railings where the luggage is stored and where there is bedding (see the Tiepolo in Vienna).

A well-known passage by Philippe de Commynes, the most ingenuous and probably the oldest description of Venice in the French language, is devoted to Fusina; I've always had such a strong affection for it that I must quote it in passing: "The day lay before me on the morning I arrived in Venice and I went as far as Chafusine [Fusina] which is five miles from Venice; there you leave the boat on which you have come, along a river, from Padua, and you climb into little boats that are very clean and covered in fine tapestries with beautiful velvet carpets inside…. The sea is extremely calm there…. You have a view of Venice and a conglomeration of houses all surrounded by water…."

The Brenta is no longer the summer-time river whose Alpine waters cooled Venice's holidaymakers; tatty huts replace the trees, the water is the colour of olive oil and on its surface float the bloated corpses of dead cats, discarded crates and empty tin cans: pylons and power lines form the dense vegetation of the new Italy; ducks attempt to swim among the plastic bottles, those latter-day water-lilies; next come a few willow trees (one understands why they weep), or reeds that resemble the plumes of the *bersaglieri*; over the water, swing bridges, looking haughty and poorly laminated, raise their metal arms for the present-day *Burchiello*, which has nothing in common with its ancestor ("Bucentaurus's grandchild", De Brosses used to say), a vessel with fifty seats, decked out in varnish, chrome and banners, and which sounds its siren impatiently from the bottom of the locks, where it is sometimes forgotten.

It is in winter that the Venetians of former times used to take refuge in the city, after the hunting season, when in November the bora had begun to blow from the heights of Grappa. The dances and public life continued until June; then people would return back along the Brenta, or go to their Palladian villas in the Euganean hills. It was in the sixteenth century that the Brenta became fashionable; each patrician family owned one or more villas there; the Pisanis had as many as fifty of them; the Contarini's residence, at Piazzola, boasted five organs, two theatres into which five horse-drawn carriages, side by side, could be driven, a lake, and enough bedrooms to house one hundred and fifty guests, as well as their servants.

The earliest fourteenth or fifteenth century engravings depict fortified, crenellated houses without windows or staircases; two or three centuries later they have become quite different sorts of dwellings, such as those we see in the Tiepolos or Longhis in the Rezzonico museum, or those in the rustic scenes in the Papadopoli gallery. The atmosphere is one of indolence, with music, siestas, ladies prattling, their husbands chatting to their servants on horseback, surrounded by a horde of friends, parasites, clavichord players, all of them gazing intently at the tables upon which piles of pewter dishes await the arrival of the food.

I don't know in what state the hundreds of villas I once visited are now in; they all used to be more or less the same, with their cast-iron gates that could not be opened because of the long grass, and their pilasters crowned with obelisks or statues of divinities wearing lichen for wigs; what has been left of them by the developers, by devaluation and by those who live in them? Only the Villa Pisani de Stra, which is maintained by the State, has its future assured. But what has become of the Psyche Room and the *trompe l'œil* ceilings of the Villa Venier; those at the Casa Widmann; the chinoiserie at the Villa Barbariga; the games room at the Villa Giustiniani; the Juno room at the Villa Grimani; all those gardens of Armida or of *The Dream of Polyphilus* and all that enchantment of the houses I once knew, some of them intact after three centuries, while others lay in ruins? And of their almond-green or pale pink drawing-rooms, the walls cracked from top to bottom, filled with ploughs and harrows and carts into which Veronese's goddesses, or the dancers of Tiepolo's minuet, have fallen from the ceiling in great slabs, rotting with damp and dilapidation?

I have over-indulged in Palladio (one can get indigestion from lean fare); this dictatorship of antiquity over three centuries, from Stockholm to the Brenta, from Lisbon to St Petersburg, and these rigid façades of Greek temples encasing a block of bricks can sometimes offend the imagination; it needs all the genius of a Gabriel,[13] allied to what is the most beautiful material in the world after Pentelic marble, Vaugirard stone, to dispel the tedium of the neo-classical.

LA MALCONTENTA

THE PRIVATELY OWNED gondolas at their moorings nod their iron prows sadly as we pass by; we disturb their slumber. The first villa at which the *Burchiello* stops is La Malcontenta. The origin of its name is obscure, it may be that a woman of the Foscari family, to whom the house belonged, was once confined there for bad behaviour, or possibly local people were unhappy about water being brought there, which meant it was taken from them.

I scarcely recognized the villa, so shaded was it by Italian poplars, those beautiful trees that grow so quickly; I had remembered a house that was dramatically isolated, and now I found it surrounded by formal lawns. It had been beautiful the way it was, it's lines intact, purified by poverty and solitude, just as the centuries had left it, ever since 1560, far away from anything, in a bare landscape, haunted by *ladri* and *rapinatori*.

Balzac set a scene there, one in which Massimilla Doni holds the handsome Emilio by the hand; hidden away between the Lagoon and the mountains, Massimilla bemoans her over-respectful lover.... Did Balzac know the Brenta, or did he have the same instinctive sense about the countryside that he had for people? His description of a Palladian *palazzo* has all the precision of those legal documents that are justifiably known as writs.

In about 1928, Catherine and Bertie had discovered La Malcontenta in the state in which it had been left after

the Austrian bombardment during the siege of 1848.
Bertie had decided to buy the villa and to restore it: an
entire lifetime would not have sufficed; lying abandoned
in the middle of cornfields, among willow trees that were
not much more than stumps, and amid pools of stagnat-
ing waters, La Malcontenta dominated the flat river
plain; initially a mountain stream, like the Isonzo, the
Mincio, the Adda or the Tagliamento, and exhausted by
its descent from the high Alps, the Brenta flattens out into
pools as it approaches the Lagoon; its dull, lack-lustre
waters, the colour of engine oil and shimmering with rust,
seem to be reluctant to reach Mestre; its banks of cracked
mud, its bridges that cast no reflection, and the impervious surface of its waters have created an unspeakable
stew that no wind can ruffle; the ancient maps trace its
course: imitating the other rivers of the Dolomites, the
Brenta displays the tentacles of an octopus encircling
Venice.

With all the patience of the eager enthusiast, but without any money, Bertie had lugged bedding, Brazilian
hammocks and tents from the upper Amazon to La
Malcontenta; Catherine, tireless, imperious, uncompro-
mising, and intent upon her futile quest, supported him
with her exuberance. At the centre point of a Latin cross
at which four rooms converged, meals were served upon
a ping-pong table that was weighed down with all the fruits
of the Rialto, on china that came from the flea-market,
while Catherine, the descendant of Vittoria Cappello
doubling as a rag and bone woman, got on with the
restoration of the building.

The parties at La Malcontenta were a bit like Plato's *Banquet* and a bit like Rabelais's Abbaye de Thélème. In rooms painted in a very soft, sometimes pinkish, light-straw colour, the guests made their way into the past through simulated doors. There was no furniture, just bales of straw for chairs, and crates. (As an anonymous visitor, yesterday I recognized the gigantic eighteenth century maps of the world, and even a portrait of Bertie.)

Once the meal was over, each of the guests kept their knives and was required to scrape down the walls in order to search for "Veronese frescoes" beneath the plaster. Had not some been found nearby, at the Villa Magnadola? I can remember José-Maria Sert, sunk into an arm-chair without springs, his two wives, Misia and Roussy, stretched out at his feet; I can see Diaghilev, a white lock detaching itself from his head of dyed hair, peering at the ceiling through a monocle attached by a ribbon, rather like a figure in Daumier's engraving *Les Amateurs de plafonds*, while Serge Lifar and Boris Kochno scraped away at the whitewashed walls. Catherine, mobilising her children as well as her lovers, past, present and future, whom she was skilful enough to make get along together, would proclaim a Veronese with every scrape of the plaster. These invisible frescoes did appear eventually, but they were not painted by the great Paolo, the *Sommo Paolo*; they were merely the work of Zelotti and Franco: *Aurora's Chamber* and *Philemon and Baucis*. I came across them again, restored and much as Henri III, the reluctant king, would have seen them on his visit to La Malcontenta on 17 July 1574. This was the occasion for the finest Venetian

festival in History; the triumphal arches were painted by
Veronese and Titian; since the sumptuary laws had been
rescinded for the occasion, patrician ladies and courtesans could be seen, followed by their servants, carrying
a hundredweight of their mistresses" pearls. It was the
moment when the Renaissance became the Baroque; in his
Histoire de Venise, Daru depicts the king, beneath the triumphal Arch that Palladio, who was dressed as a Venetian
senator, had erected to him. Glassmakers, aboard a raft, are
at work at their blowing while the twenty-three-year-old
monarch looks on, marvelling at a sea-monster spitting
fire through its nostrils.[14] Henri III was so impressed by the
glassworkers of Murano that he ennobled their corpora-
tion and spent a fortune on mirrors and chandeliers; to
pay for them, he borrowed one hundred thousand écus
from La Serenissima, which caused the Pope to remark:
"There go écus that the people of Venice will never see
again." You don't have to go far to look at this triumphant Henri III, these days he is at the Jacquemart-
André museum, having made the journey for you from
La Malcontenta to Boulevard Haussmann.

La Malcontenta was home to those dozen or so legendary men and women of whom, Jean-Louis, Lifar and
Kochno apart, no one is left;[15] they are gone forever,
through the simulated doors of the drawing-room. Misia
Sert ("When I was twenty, I used to see her at her father,
the sculptor Godebski's house," my father used to say, "a
beautiful panther, imperious, bloodthirsty and frivolous."),
Misia, not the woman who emerges from her flimsy
Mémoires, but the one who existed: effervescing with joy or

fury, eccentric, acquisitive and a collector of geniuses, all of whom were in love with her: Vuillard, Bonnard, Renoir, Stravinsky, Picasso… a collector of hearts and of Ming trees in pink quartz; whenever her latest fads were launched, they became instantly fashionable among all her followers, and were exploited by designers, written about by journalists and imitated by every empty-headed society lady. Misia, the queen of modern baroque, who organised her life around nacre, pearls and the bizarre; the sullen and deceitful Misia, who would bring together friends who did not know one another "in order to then make them quarrel", according to Proust. Brilliant in her treachery and subtle in her cruelty, Philippe Berthelot used to say of Misia that one should never entrust her with anything: "Here comes the cat, hide your birds," he would say whenever she rang the doorbell. In her *boutique fantasque* on the quai Voltaire, she kindled genius in the same way that certain kings can create victors, by her magnetic presence alone, through an unseen oscillation of a branch of her hazel tree. Misia was as strong as the life-force that smouldered within her; she was mean yet generous, she devoured people in their thousands, she was cajoling, mischievous, subtle, mercenary, even more of a Mme Verdurin than the original one, and she esteemed and despised men and women at a glance. There was the Misia of the Symbolists' Paris, of Fauvist Paris, First World War Paris, the Paris of the Versailles Peace Treaty, the Paris of Venice. Dissatisfied Misia was as well padded as a sofa, yet if you craved rest, she was a sofa who was likely to send you packing. Misia dissatisfied had piercing eyes which laughed even though her mouth was already beginning to pout.

Where this all-devouring creature was concerned, rapture was followed by disgust, a yes by a no, just as thunder follows lightning; with her, you had to perform quickly.

Serge Lifar at the exhibition celebrating twenty years of the Ballets Russes at the Pavillon de Marsan, 1939

1929

A T THE SLUICE-GATES of Venetian houses you reveal all about yourself the moment you set foot in the doorway. "A slippery city," D.H.Lawrence said of her. I had arrived there the day after Diaghilev had died. I thought once more about the life of this brilliant impresario whose love of art had been his driving force; he was much more of a sorcerer than an impresario and he had the wizardry of an electro-magnet; his intelligence was not sufficiently developed that it outshone his sense of discovery; his secret derived from the fact that he only ever thought of his own pleasure, requiring the approval of merely a handful of people, such as Picasso, Stravinsky, Lady Ripon, Misia…; totally indifferent to the fashions of the day, he never took peeps through the hole in the stage curtain; and he never took a penny on the side. Only his somnambulism can explain his temerity, his inability to foresee obstacles, his crazy improvisations and the way he was blinded to all but his own destiny (The final act of *Petrushka* was created only ten minutes before the curtain went up at the dress rehearsal).

I reflected on Serge's career from that moment in 1904 when Prince Volkonsky, the director of the Imperial Theatres, parted with the services of the very young choreographer, criticising him for having staged *Sylvia* "with too many of his personal ideas", up until his death in Venice; I thought about his revolutionary yet classical destiny, about this harbourer of monsters, who arrived in

Paris and scattered his Muscovite seed there, giving new birth to painting, music, song and dance. I thought of the Ballets Russes which, as a humble soldier arriving by train at the Gare Saint-Lazare, I would watch from the gods at the Châtelet or the Opéra. Diaghilev slips through my past like a stag in the forest; "I caught sight of him" say the stalkers; but how often did I catch glimpses of Serge! I had known the triumphant Diaghilev from the Châtelet in 1910 to London in 1913, before coming across him, four years later, reduced to poverty (he was never rich) in Spain; impervious to boos and catcalls, he had an Ancien Régime courtesy which storms would occasionally ruffle when some drama or other broke out in the seraglio; beneath the Russian demeanour, the China-man was always slumbering.... Cosmopolitan in appearance, but Russian in his soul, everywhere he went he recreated that eschatological, Byzantine atmosphere of the eternal Russia; the triumphs, the downfalls, the debts, the harassment, the beloved bodies sewn into sacks and tossed into the Bosphorus; pitting Nijinsky against Fokine, Benoit against Bakst, Lifar against Massine, in a storm of champagne, delirious telegrams, fancy food and dried bread, accompanied by assurances of happiness and threats of suicide, and, finally, his fatal diabetes which was treated with ten dishes that were forbidden him; such was Serge, that tortured executioner. 1929 was not just the year of his death, but a year of wonderful immunity, of a certain freedom about the way one dressed, of the sort of pleasures that were greater than pleasure itself; it marked the end of that wandering chivalry, of that secret intelligence between members of a sect ... one that never really existed. Diaghilev was forbidden a residence permit during the First World War; he was even treated suspiciously in the countries that were neutral, up until the moment when he charmed Alfonso XIII, to whom he introduced the young Picasso, who had painted the sets for *Parade*. In the spring of 1918, we used to lunch together daily at the "Palace" in Madrid; Massine had left him to go to Barcelona to be given lessons in Spanish dancing, and I was the only confidant Diaghilev had; I can still hear him recounting his unbelievable misfortunes; how the Ballets Russes's costumes and stage sets had been sunk off Cadiz—the sort of wreck that might have occurred in *Candide*; how what was saved from the wreckage had been destroyed in a fire in South America; how Clemenceau had barred his entry into France. (Powerless, for once, Misia had been unable to procure a visa for him; Philippe Berthelot was in disgrace and she had not yet won over Mandel.) In 1920, I came across Diaghilev again; he was back in Paris and he had already had time to explore the latest paintings and to have chosen the best of them, never making a mistake and never allowing a source to run dry.

On the 19th of August 1929, a few days before my arrival, the ceremonial floating bier that is used for funeral processions in Venice ferried the magician's mortal remains to the funeral island of San Michele. Lifar threw himself into the grave. Whenever I see a funeral procession on its way to San Michele, with the priest in charge of the ceremony standing behind the gondolier at

Serge Diaghilev's tomb on the island of San Michele, Venice

the stern, the funeral director at the prow, and with the silver Lion of St Mark concealing its affliction beneath its folded wings, I think of Diaghilev, that indefatigable man, lying at rest.

Death would not quell the storm in which Diaghilev lived; his death throes had imposed a truce upon irreconcilable passions; it was broken the moment he breathed his last; at the foot of his bed, the two friends who had looked after him immediately hurled themselves upon one another. I was given an account of his final moments by the three women who were present, Misia, Chanel and the Baronne Émile d'Erlanger.

As Byron wrote to Murray, from Venice, on the 25th of November 1816: "Love, in this part of the world, is not a sinecure."

1929

A FEW OF THE SURROUNDINGS had changed: on the Lido there were now a huge number of beach huts, those symbols of social prestige that are what the boxes at La Scala were in Stendhal's time. The iron Accademia Bridge had been covered in a wooden construction, in the manner of Carpaccio or Bellini; the Palazzo Franchetti had acquired a lawn.

From having struck their bell so frequently, in my absence, the arms of the two Moors—the *Mori*—who chime the hour at the Mercerie, had grown very stiff.

THE ISLAND OF SAN LAZZARO

E VER SINCE the Lido began to rival Saint-Tropez, the contrast of this beach with the island of San Lazzaro, a stone's throw away, has become ever more striking. After the hell of the summer, one finds the calm of prayer; one savours every moment spent beneath the magnolias, at the centre of the cloister, which seem to repeat itself like the beads of a rosary. La Serenissima gave this little island to the Armenian Mekhitarist monks when they arrived from Crete, where they had been driven out by the Turks, and they found a refuge here, far from the sunburnt, shaven legs and those infra-red cooked chickens. An Armenian patron has just provided the monastery with a large octagonal building, shaped like a church dome and built with air-conditioning, in which to keep their manuscripts; all that remains of a very great civilization; we never realised that a civilization would be able to be conserved in a room half the size of the reading room in the Bibliothèque Nationale! The Armenian rite, like the Orthodox, knew and recognised the value of mystery: a curtain conceals the celebrant (a velvet curtain, woven in gold, a gift from the late Queen Margherita of Italy); thrice, at the Consecration, and before and after Communion, the priest disappears from the congregations' view; God is the winner.

I had not set foot in the Armenian monastery for fifty years; for such an ancient civilization, that was a mere flash. The cypress trees had grown taller and the sea breezes had turned them brown, while the Melchite Friars, their "beards the colour of meteors" (*Byron*), had grown white; their cemetery had doubled in size. This Eastern Catholic rite, divided as Venice is, and as I myself am, between East and West, between the Roman faith and Orthodoxy, was given refuge here after the defeat of Morosini in Morea, in the seventeenth century. Along with Vienna and Etchmiadzin, the home of these monks with their black habits remains a famous centre for Byzantine studies. Napoleon, who closed down the monasteries, respected these Venetian anchorites; was he preserving them for the fulfilment of his oriental dream?

I feel grateful to them for being the first importers of angora cats to the West.

PROUST AT THE ARMENIAN
MONASTERY

THREE TIMES A WEEK, Byron rowed from Venice to San Lazzaro, where he came to learn Armenian; in the visitor's book, we read, alongside his signature: "Byron, English". (He despised England, but he was proud of her when he was abroad.) Proust, in his turn, would come to add his name to the register in the spring of 1900; not being a nostalgic exile, he did not put "French" after his name.

It is hard to believe that in late 1919 Proust still had difficulties in placing an article about Venice in the newspapers, hoping humbly that "it would be accepted". Throughout his life, Proust promised himself trips to Venice; when the Great War was over, he used to say, he hoped to be able to return there with Vaudoyer or with me, once his book was completed; he had dreamed about the city for a long time, ever since childhood, just like his grandmother who, in her case, never went there; he thought about it when he spent the autumn at Evian, in early September, when the Lake of Geneva takes on a Lombardian softness and seems to grow more like the Borromée islands, from which it is barely separated by the once impassable mass of the Simplon, now easily crossed or tunnelled through; the same summer palaces, the same clarity of its shores, the same *truite au bleu* colour of its morning surfaces.

Proust had a special feeling for Venice (and not just for those neckties from *Au Carnaval de Venise*, on the Boulevard des Capucines, which Charles Haas bought). How could he escape from the World Exhibition,[16] he wondered, how could he travel to the magical city on his own, when he was so ill? He needed a companion, but he couldn't find one; one of his letters, dated October 1899, is nothing but a cry from the heart for Venice. Why didn't Emmanuel or Antoine Bibesco—the two nephews of the famous composer, at whose home, the Villa Bessaraba at Amphion, Proust so often stayed—why didn't one of them go along as his guide? Italy was only three hours away.... In early May 1900, Proust learnt that Reynaldo Hahn and his cousin Marie Nordlinger were in Rome and would be going on to Venice. He couldn't stand it any longer and persuaded Mme Proust to accompany him; in the train, after they had passed Milan, she translated Ruskin for him....

In the index to the Pléiade edition of *À la recherche*, there are a hundred listings for Venice; we see Proust so intoxicated by this city which he had finally conquered that he had forgotten his dreaded fevers: a young man exhilarated by the splendour of St Mark's; a Marcel who astonished his mother because he found the strength to be up at ten o'clock in the morning, etc.[17]

The month of May came and went; the Proustian acid combined marvellously well with the Venetian base. *La Fugitive* contains a hundred divers impressions in which Venice merges or fuses with Combray (the function of the houses in the Grand-Rue compared to that of the palaces, the relationship between the sunlight playing upon the awnings on the canal and those on the family drapery shop, the comparison of the Danieli Hotel and Aunt Léonie's home, etc.). The *Conversation avec Maman* in *Contre Sainte-Beuve*, reveals further recollections: "At lunchtime, when my gondola brought me back, I noticed Mamma's shawl upon the alabaster balustrade", etc.

These memories from *Contre Sainte-Beuve* precede those in *La Fugitive*; what they have in common is that they both mention a tiff between mother and son that has always intrigued me, a curious quarrel which, considering that this disagreement was to have such lasting overtones, one would like to be able to shed some light upon; the odd thing about them is that *Contre Sainte-Beuve*, which was published first (although it is difficult to establish a firm date, since it is made up of fragments collected together between 1905 and 1909), tells us about "an evening when, spitefully, after a quarrel with Mamma, I told her that I was leaving (Venice).... I had given up my idea of leaving, but I wanted to spin out Mamma's sadness at believing that I had left". It is the son, therefore, who in this instance wants to return to Paris (but since his mother has only come to Venice for his sake, one fails to understand why she did not yield to her son's wish to return)... whereas, later, in *La Fugitive*, in which the visit to Venice is treated at greater length, the situation is reversed; this time, it is the Narrator who refuses to leave Venice and return to Paris with his mother: "My mother had decided that we should leave ... my plea (to remain) aroused in my nerves, stimulated by the Venetian springtime, that old desire to resist ... that determination to fight which once used to drive me to impose my own will brutally upon those I loved most." We know what ensued: having allowed his mother to leave for the station, the Narrator rushes after her and catches up with her just before the train is about to depart; it's a long way from the Danieli to the Stazione, but the surge of filial affection shortens the journey. The umbilical cord remains uncut once more.

This new account of a conflict between mother and son seems closer to reality than the earlier one. For Proust, Venice is the city of his unconscious (1900 style).

Each of us has his *dead-weights*; the best known are perhaps the least obscure, those one can get away from. Proust, the very image of the introvert, contrasted with that exemplar of the extrovert, Casanova.

Where was the Venice of Proust if not within his own self? Throughout the whole of *À la recherche*, Venice continues to be the symbol of freedom, of his freeing himself from his mother, in the first place, and from Albertine later on; "Venice is the image of what passion prevents him from realising"; Albertine conceals Venice from him almost as if love was blocking out all other joys.

In reality, Proust returned to Paris in late May 1900, with his mother. In the autumn, he took his revenge; stubbornly determined, he went back to Venice, alone this time, just as he had wanted to do. He stayed there for ten days in October 1900, not at the Danieli, but at the Hôtel de l'Europe, opposite the Salute. "This mysterious visit," writes Painter. Psychologically, perhaps, but not in a literary sense, since *La Fugitive* has given us some celebrated passages, describing the Narrator's solitary wanderings "through humble *campi* and little abandoned *rii*", in an ardent search for Venetian girls, "alone … in the middle of the enchanted city, like a character in the *Arabian Nights*".

Proust was the masked prince of a Serenissima that was far from serene, of a Venice that was very different to the city of banquets, ceremonies and fanfares that had greeted Adrien Proust, Marcel's father, in October 1892, when as a professor of hygiene he had represented France at an international health conference that took place in Venice.

For peace of mind, I thought as I left San Lazzaro, better to choose another city to the androgynous Venice, "where you never know where the land ends, or where the water begins", as Elstir tells Albertine.

THREE VENETIAN CAFÉS

OVER THE YEARS, three Venetian cafés have remained unchanged for me. In the mornings, it's the one at the foot of the Accademia, under the shelter of the bridge; the glass of orange juice is on a level with the Canal. At about ten o'clock, the sun is facing you; the air is still fresh and its invigorating breeze is blown straight from the sea. Seated at this little café, almost beneath the arch of the bridge, I'm reading *See Venice and Die* by James Hadley Chase. It's in the "Série Noire" series, that last refuge of the romantic.... "With one hand, Don seized his adversary by the throat; with the other, he delivered a hook to the jaw; Curzio fell into the canal...."

In this secretive republic, where smothered bodies are found weighted down or are drowned discreetly off Sant'Ariano, such brutal uppercuts direct to the body ring a bizarre bell. There is a symmetry there that adds spice to the antithesis.

At night-time my café is at La Fenice. The little piazza contains two churches, the theatre, a large restaurant and the theatre bar. Something of everything has been performed in this square, from Carlo Gozzi to Georges Courteline. A thick curtain of white polygonums conceal the lanterns and filters the smoke from the bar full of hippies, with their vague, drugged expressions, looking like frogmen who have been forgotten beneath the water. The square is lit by projectors which darken the ribbon of sky and cause the sheen of the stone to dazzle and the columns to loom out of the shadow; it's between God and the Muses as to who has most to boast about; everything here has been created by man, for man; everything is so well balanced, so well accommodated over the invisible water below and all the plans so harmoniously compatible that you feel as happy as you do when you're drunk.

When the weather is scorching hot, there is another café, on the Campo San Zanipolo, where you can take a siesta behind the pages of the *Gazzettino* without being disturbed. Above you is the Colleone statue, and behind, the Ospedale; to left and to right is the church of Santi Giovanni e Paolo, the Gothic pantheon of the most famous doges, Mocenigo, Morosini, Loredan, as well as the tomb of Sebastian Venier, who commanded the fleet at Lepanto, thus avenging that poor Bragadin to whom the Senate erected a monument, in this very nave, as consolation for his having been so badly treated by the Turks. In Eastern countries, there is no more unforgivable crime than to pose as a victor when one has been defeated. In the sixteenth century, Famagusta, exhausted by a lengthy siege, surrendered to the Turk. The Venetian admiral, Marcantonio Bragadin, the defender of the city, gave himself up to the pasha who very courteously invited him to dine. Bragadin, with an escort of great magnificence, arrived at the banquet beneath a red silk parasol, the Asiatic symbol of suzerainty. The pasha was so deeply offended that he had Bragadin arrested before he left the table; the admiral's nose and ears were chopped off; his execution was postponed three times; for ten days running he was hauled before the pasha and made to kiss the ground; after which, he was flayed alive (*scorticato vivo*); his corpse, stuffed with straw, was paraded through the city on a cow, before being dried and shipped to the arsenal in Constantinople.

After the battle of Lepanto, the Venetians recaptured the city. Today, Bragadin lies in this beautiful Gothic nave of Santi Giovanni e Paolo.

In the seventeenth century, another Bragadin was caught slipping a note intended for the Spanish ambassador into a crack in a church bench and was hanged between two columns in the Piazzetta. A third and no less unfortunate Bragadin, an alchemist, had tried to sell the Doge a recipe for making gold; he was imprisoned, but escaped and fled to Bavaria, where he hoodwinked thousands of people and lived like a king. In Munich, the executioner decapitated him with a two-handed sword.

A century later, it was yet another Bragadin, a former Inquisitor, who became the young Casanova's first guardian; on the pretext of teaching him the cabbala, Casanova used to hoodwink him.

From the corner of my little Zanipolo café I can see Colleone; at whom is this piercingly defiant gaze directed, at his contemporaries or posterity? How could such a resolute, well established captain have managed to possess such unpredictable supporters that he exchanged them as often as he changed his shirt? (even in his own time, it was said of the *condottieri* that they were splendid fighters, but that "they never got much blood on their shirts"). The whole of this great rascal's life was spent fighting for Venice against Milan, or for Sforza against the Council of Ten; they do not appear to have held this against him, because every time he deserted them the *condottiere* came back to renew his offers. It is hard to put oneself into the fifteenth century frame of mind; (even in our age of mercenaries): how can those fine heads, whose images Donatello, Uccello, Antonello da Messina, La Francesca and Vinci have bequeathed to us, have been those of ordinary military leaders, without any of them being killed? Do they lie, this terrible face of the Bergamask, this supercilious head, these hawk's eyes, this unforgiving mouth, this sly expression? Should the credit go to Colleone himself, or to his band of adventurers who were all the more loyal to him because he looked after his men and paid them well; better than he was himself; we can see from his accounts which survive that the Senate of Venice quibbled over his pay, ducat for ducat, only discharging their obligations after long delays, having first tried to obtain a reduction (each did his best to swindle the other).

These *condottieri*, whose fame has endured for three centuries, were worth their wages; in Northern Italy, at the end of the fifteenth century, there was a veritable market in bands, *milizie* who could be bought, gangs of adventurers that could be hired by the hour or at a flat rate and who priced themselves very highly, even abroad. Louis XI and Charles le Téméraire spent a long time fighting for Colleone's assistance, offering more and more money to the doge to sub-contract him to them, which caused embarrassment to the Republic, for they did not want to offend such great princes.

ONCE UPON a time, the Venice *Gazzettino* published a list of people who had fallen into the water during the day; this column was withdrawn. Are less people falling in?

Everything used to be original and different here: the Serenissima had her own calendar that began on the 1st of March; the days were counted from the time of the sunset.

The real enemy of Venice has not been the Turk, but the Italian from the mainland; the wars against the Infidel enriched the Republic; the wars against Milan or the Pope ruined her.

People rode on horseback in Venice up until the fourteenth century. On the piazza where Colleone gambols, there was once a riding school with seventy-five horses.

So as to ward off the Muslims, the two Christian merchants who stole the body of St Mark from Alexandria in Egypt in order to take it back to Venice, had the idea of burying the relic in a carcass of salted pork.

That black little canal; at the far end, at the very top of the perspective, there is a house of a dull red colour; as the sun goes down, its beams suddenly alight on the façade and illuminate it just as one lights a candle.

Water lends a depth to the sounds, a silky retentiveness that can last for over a minute; it is as if one was sinking into the depths.

Emerging from the Sansovino Library, where the courtyard has been glazed and turned into a reading room, I go through a door which opens on to the Procuraties, between two giants whose knees are at the height of my face. The sun is setting on the Ponte della Paglia; in the background is San Giorgio Maggiore, which the big liners steaming hurriedly through the channels before nightfall look as if they will sweep away as they pass.

The Paris newspapers have just arrived; it is six o'clock. Caught in the light of the setting sun, the mosaics of St Mark's glisten like a thousand-year-old set of kitchen utensils.

In Venice, man has discovered a new joy: not having a car, as once at Zermatt, and, once upon a time, in Bermuda, and he is happy in a city without pavements, without traffic lights,[18] without whistles, where one walks along as smoothly as the flowing waters: as I set out, I feel just like a ball, without specific gravity.

The houses of Venice are buildings that have a nostalgic longing to be boats: this is why their ground floors are often flooded. They are satisfying their fondness for a permanent home as well as their nomadic instincts.

Venice is the most expensive city in Italy, but the true pleasures she offers cost nothing: one hundred lira for the *vaporetto*, from the Lido to the station, by the *accelerato*, that is to say by the slowest service.

Pretentious householders give each other trees here.

The troops of the Directoire planted a tree of Liberty at the entrance to the ghetto.

Midday; everyone stops talking; Venetian mouths are full of spaghetti; so much seafood accompanies it that the noodles turn into seaweed.

The shop selling seashells to collectors, at the corner of rue du Dauphin.

In Venice, *una sposa* is not a married woman, but the wife to be; they cut corners.

A person's life frequently resembles those *palazzi* on the Grand Canal where the lower floors were begun with an array of stones carved in the shapes of diamonds, and whose upper floors were hastily completed with dried mud.

Like an old lady on crutches, Venice is dependent on a forest of posts; a million of them were needed just to underpin the Salute; and that was not enough.

In very bad weather, in St Mark's Square, the waters rise up through the joints in the paving stones; it reminds me of the Nouveau circus, in the rue du Faubourg-Saint-Honoré, which, once the show was over, became a swimming-pool.

At Chioggia, the sails of the fishing boats have the same red paintings on red backgrounds as on Inca shrouds....

The *palazzi* on the Grand Canal, with their belts of blackened seaweed and barnacles.

These Leicas, these Zeiss; do people no longer have eyes?

Of all the *traghetti*, the most charming is that of Santa Maria del Giglio, with its gondoliers who play cards beneath the red virgin vines in October. You have to wait until a hand of piquet is over before daring to climb on board.

Squeezed into the *rii* of Venice like a bookmark between the pages; certain streets are so narrow that Browning used to complain that he could not open his umbrella in them.

The finest location for a shoe-shine boy is at the exit from the Mercerie. While he polishes, this is what you

see: the flight lines of St Mark's, lined with the ogives of
the Doges' Palace; in the foreground, the two porphyry
lions polished for a thousand years by the stirrup-less trot-
ting of young Venetians; to the right, the Campanile casts
its shadow over my foot. At the far end of the perspective,
like a backdrop, San Giorgio Maggiore, immense … until
an oil tanker interposes itself, reducing the scale to the
image of a painting at the bottom of a plate; the bows of
the tanker, which is more vast than the church, are already
level with the Danieli, whereas the stern has scarcely
passed the Dogana.

Venice has run herself aground in a place that was forbidden: therein lay her genius.

The Venetians invented income tax, statistics, state pen-
sions, book censorship, the lottery, the ghetto and glass
mirrors.

Montaigne called on a literary courtesan who read him
an endless elegy on her work; Montaigne would have
done better to catch the pox.

The cats are the vultures of Venice.

During the seventeenth century, following an earthquake, the Grand Canal ran dry for two hours.

Colleone's horse: one might criticise Verrocchio for the
tail, which is a little low. And how could the horseman
have achieved that raising of the forearm when his spurs
are so far from the horse's girth?

That box for anonymous denunciations that was placed
at the entrance to the Doges' Palace, and which has a lion's
mouth at its opening, is famous; the inquisitors put those
bocche di leone not just in the Palace, but in every district of

the city. It is not lions that should figure on the Serenissima's coat of arms, but vipers.

Duse's first role was that of Cosetta.... (*Festival of
Theatre*, Venice, 1969).

Who was it who described Reynaldo Hahn in Venice
thus: "An upright piano, a great deal of smoke, a little
music"?

A Parisian man of letters. In 1834, as he disembarked
at the Danieli, where did Alfred de Musset run off to? To
the Missiglia reading room, to see whether La Revue des
Deux Mondes had arrived.

Springtime: let others repaint the fronts of their houses;
in March, a Venetian first of all scrapes the bottom of his
gondola.

Where better than Venice can Narcissus contemplate
himself?

Wagner, listening to his own music, at the Café
Quadri...

A Venetian never visits the rest of Italy.[19]

The Venetian dialect is distinguished by the letter Z;
the Grand Canal itself is shaped like a Z.

1934

"VENICE, the mask of Italy" (*Byron*).
    In front of the Scuola San Marco, I come across
Fulgence, accompanied by Bernardine, his wife; they
are staying near the Accademia.

Taking me to one side:

"I've moved Françoise into the Lido and I've persuaded Coralie to conceal herself in Padua", Fulgence
confesses to me. "My two ladies don't know one another,
fortunately. As for me, I'm keeping Venice to myself,
with Bernardine."

The fire-guard of marriage…

1934

HEARD ABOUT the death of Stavisky in Venice. The USSR joins the UN. Death of King Albert and the assassination of Dollfuss. Night of the Long Knives. Hindenburg. Hitler master of Germany. Publication of *L'Armée de métier*, by de Gaulle, with an introduction by Pétain.

How does one find these facts in the treasury of History? The doge threw his ring into the sea; who would have thought that fisherman would discover this ring in a fish's belly, and that one day we would be able to see it in the Treasury of St Mark's?

At the Institut, I come across an ancient and delightful paper by the Comte de Mas Latrie: *De l'empoisonnement politique dans la république de Venise*; from which it emerges that people were assassinated at the Doges' Palace up until the second half of the eighteenth century; not only did the Senate frequently appear to be interested in the proposals of the pirates, but it let it be known and discussed advance payments, which varied according to the person who was to be eliminated, a sultan or a simple Albanian chieftain. Who provided the poison, and what was it?

At which point, nineteenth century Venetian scholars reply to French accusations: "What about your kings? What about Louis XI? Did not your François I wish for the death of Pope Clement VII? Our word *potione* (a potion) has a double meaning in French: it's '*poison*'…"

THE RIALTO MARKET

D ESPITE THE ROLLING and swaying, the peaches in
their baskets do not move; they're plump and ined-
ible. As for the fish, they're not very big, with the exception of the tuna and swordfish, but what a tang of the
high seas! They were caught the previous day and are
untouched by ice and gamma rays, and have not been
brushed with penicillin; after Greece, England, La Rochelle
and the Hanseatic ports, after Antwerp, Portugal and
Venice, fish from anywhere else seems tasteless.

Herbs, little used elsewhere, play an important part in
Italian cooking, and they are sold by toothless old herbal-
ists; a fusion of plucked leaves, sedge from the marshes,
sweet watercress, lemon balm, edible lichens; ten vari-
eties of chervil, limitless amounts of mint, oregano, mar-
joram and little seasoning bags which, once they are
crushed, make up the sauces, such as that *salsa verde* one
adds to boiled dishes, that is unknown even in Provence.

In the years that I lived far away from Venice, Denise
would bring me back gondolier's shoes, made of black
velvet and with rope soles; you could buy them at the
Rialto for a few lire; her two Charles, both elegant creatures, would wear nothing else.

1931

In 1816 Countess Albrizzi gave a ball here at which Byron fell in love with Teresa Gamba, Countess Guiccioli; he had first met her three months earlier; three months of incubation, then, on that evening, the mutual *coup de foudre*.

What followed is well-known: Guiccioli, in love and consumptive, took refuge in Ravenna, where her elderly husband (there were fifty years between them) took all the blame upon himself, and where the Countess's father, Count Gamba, came to beg Byron not to abandon his beloved daughter, who was coughing herself to death. The reason I am recalling this famous affair is in order to repeat Byron's final words; exasperated (particularly since he found himself dragged into a political conspiracy involving the Italian family) Byron sighed: "I only wanted to be her escort; how could I have known that this affair would turn into an English novel?" (that is to say domestic and tearful).

Lauzun and Ligne were merely witty; Byron transcribed Italian buffoonery into English humour; the epigrammatic retorts in Wilde's plays are to be found in every line of the poet's correspondence: "The women here have abominable notions about constancy…" and (departing for Missolonghi): "I prefer to love a cause than to love a woman." When Cocteau, who was asked what he would like to take away with him if his house caught fire, replied: "I'd take away the fire", he sounds just like the Byron of the *Letters*.

"Why were there ten thousand gondolas four centuries ago, and five hundred today?"

"The job's a dead loss! (It's as if you were listening to a Paris cab driver.) The season is too short.... A gondola costs a million lire.... *Vaporetti* and *lance*, they break your arms with the wash they make.... You risk your life at every turning.... On the Grand Canal they come at you like a bull in a china shop...."

"But you're singing?"

"So as to forget..."

The gondolier tells me that ever since the seventeenth century a gondola's blade has had five prongs; the gondola's reflection quivers over the waters that are mottled with sunshine and oil.

Three o'clock in the morning.

At this hour, with no one about, Venice is like a Guardi painting.

No more *funiculi*.

Were it not for the television aerials, one could be in the eighteenth century.

Nothing ruffles the surface of the water apart from a foul-smelling gust from the direction of the Dogana, where the ripples are caused by a puff of wind which does not reach me.

In ten minutes the *peotta*, the large gondola that collects the rubbish, will pass by on its way to the Giudecca. Venice is creating new islands out of refuse, making the most of her waste material.

When the first motorboat speeds past, the reflections of mooring posts look like crooked, Solomonic columns.

151

1925–1969

A CRUISE IN VENICE

I CAN REMEMBER a farewell party at sea, some forty years ago. The *Zara*, a vessel of 500 tons, with its black hull and gold lines, and flying the American flag, was anchored off the Doges' Palace, ready to take us to Asia Minor. There were not many of us, just five passengers; a wise choice. Half of Venice, then a small provincial town, flocked on board and stayed so late that we missed the tide; for a month we were obliged to drink water, since the ship's cellars had run dry. The captain, an Englishman, almost died.

As I recall that noisily celebrated departure, I ask myself in what way did a rather fashionable cruise like that one differ from those that serve as the background to modern novels. (I don't regret having mixed in the society of those times; it meant that I didn't have to spend my later life doing so, as Valéry or Gide did; it's all experience.)

The pleasures of life in the twenties were uninhibited, but one had to be well dressed and come from a good family; there was none of that American-inspired brutality, no cold wars or hot ones, no world of pressure groups, alcohol, drugs, machine guns and erotic films. Survival? We were still learning about good manners. It was the Americans who were Europeanised; not the other way round.

People knew how to behave, even when playing the most reckless of games, those that have always existed; the scandals that took place in certain of the *palazzi* on the

Grand Canal didn't even reach the hotel bars; during an evening on board ship, when local society had gathered, you wouldn't find any political agents, or betting clerks, or well-connected antique dealers without a license, or young women filling out their monthly wages in the gossip columns of unsavoury newspapers; the likes of couturiers, perfume sellers and suppliers had scarcely begun to mix socially with their clientele. Everybody still wore the clothes of their profession: pederasts offered themselves exclusively to males, without earning bits on the side from elderly ladies; Whites were simply less dark than Blacks, debauched old witches, celebrated for their weaknesses, did not publish their edifying memoirs, priests did not look like Protestant pastors, sociology students did not disguise themselves as Kurdish shepherds, and Kurdish shepherds as parachutists. Never could the current expression "to be out of sorts" be better translated than by our contemporary transvestites.

One never saw one's hostess getting up from table between courses, taking photographs of her guests herself for some illustrated weekly, and then reclaiming her expenses. The prying snapshot, with the blackmailing photographer entering through the kitchens (as at the Labia), hiding beneath the bed and testing the very limits of the law, was unknown; this all stemmed from an American businesswoman who gave cut-price parties and, a few years later, fetched up in Europe.

Another difference was the police; the last nations to be highly civilized had not yet acquired police forces; there was Austrian surveillance in Stendhal's time, Mosca hiding among the double basses at the theatre in Parma and the Italian gendarmerie, those brave *carabinieri* with their red plumes, but that was all; our information networks did not exist yet; neither did directories for each of the ministries, the "contacts" for the different weapons, the secret services attached to the most tropical of embassies, the investigation bureaux of the large banks, newspaper and magazine spies, syndicates on the look-out, files of casinos, jewellers and palaces. It is about our own time that Gérard de Nerval might have spoken of a "gang of privileged robbers"; it's not *Cosmopolis* that Paul Bourget would have written today, but *Interpol*.

Having said this, there are a good number of similarities between a cruise in the 1920s and one today; you get away from the fogs, but become involved instead in disputes. Our voyage ended badly: as soon as we entered the Mediterranean, the family who had invited us began to quarrel among themselves; the poet on board had a premonition of a storm and disembarked at Bursa, and two other guests got off at Naples, so as not to have to take sides between the aunt and her niece. Left on their own, the members of the family locked themselves away in their cabins; as soon as they got back to Venice, they turned their backs on one another and never saw each other again; do they speak to one another from beyond the grave?

VENICE, SEPTEMBER 1930

O N THE 24TH OF SEPTEMBER 1930, I found myself sitting on a stone bench overlooking the lagoon. There where once the *Bucintoro*, its golden stern lighting up the primordial waters like the sun, and the Serenissima's fleet lay at anchor—the ships flecked crimson, their long oars making them look like boiled lobsters—ten grey torpedo boats were lined up. The autumn sky trembled as the triangular shapes of the seaplanes approached; red, green and white tricolor pennants hung down to the ground (with all that ancient sense of "drapery" that flags have still retained in Italy); sailors from the Venetian battleships walked past, their eyes shining like copper. Officers wearing scarves and gold sword-knots passed with confident footstep to report for duty.

Venice, the city of Nietzsche, was instructing the new Italy: "Men must be given back the courage of their natural instincts" … "national narrow-mindedness, military strictness, a better physiology, space, meat …" I am back in front of St Mark's, just as I was twenty years ago. Why did I buy *La Volonté de puissance* yesterday? What coincidence made me open it at the chapter entitled "*Contre Rousseau*"? "Unfortunately man is no longer wicked enough…" "It is lassitude and moralism that are the curse."

The winged lion is proof that the future of Italy lies with the sea. St Mark versus the Orient, Manin[20] versus Austria, Wagner and Nietzsche. In the *Berliner Tageblatt*, which I bought beneath the Procuraties, I read the words of Hitler, curt as a machine-gun: "If needs be, heads will fall."

14-24 September: ten days were enough. Hitler's voice once more, at Leipzig: "I shall introduce a vast spiritual upheaval" ... and the National Socialists' manifesto: "We shall use iron restraint against all who oppose the material and spiritual rebuilding of the nation."

I look around me and I notice the blond creatures with bare knees who have descended from the Tyrol upon St Mark's Square. The youth of 1930 are beginning to be seen everywhere and to make their loud voices heard. It is a Germany that no longer reads *All Quiet on the Western Front,* that speaks of "real wars, which will stop all forms of frivolity"; a hot-blooded age that has not experienced suffering: the students who have elected Hitler are former Communist sympathisers.

"We are entering a tragic period," Nietzsche foretold, "a catastrophic age."

1936

YESTERDAY MUSSOLINI brought Hitler to Napoleon's headquarters at Stra. Behind them lay Treviso, the first foothills of the Dolomites and Mount Grappa. In front of them, the Euganean Hills that served Giorgione's backdrop. Lichen-covered statues cast their drowning cries into the sea of shining magnolias. Ochre-coloured sails, pierced by an eye flushed red with conjunctivitis, pass by, Dutch style, at the level of the cornfields.

Twenty years ago, Padua was an ancient university city, drowsing over its degrees; today, she has come to life again and the surrounding marshland has been dried out; the Paduans are learning their good manners from the walls: "*Well brought-up people do not swear.*" (I immediately make up a list of all the swear-words I can remember.) I also read: "*Spitting is a custom of the past*"; instantly, this leads me to wonder: why did our forebears spit? Is salivating any more unhealthy? Does expectorating get rid of phlegm any more effectively?

The education of the masses; ten years earlier, in Moscow, I watched schoolchildren being taught to brush their teeth up and down, and not from side to side.

1935

"KILL THE FLIES!" (One of Mussolini's recommenda-tions.)[21]

1935

For the fascists, Othello was not a coloured man; he was a *More*, which does not mean a Moor, but a native of Morea. The original Othello was the Doge Cristoforo Moro.

On the Piazzetta, every male nowadays has the chin of Colleone and the look of a Guatamelata.

1937

RAIMONDO, the *maître d'hôtel* at the Splendid, has watched Europe parade along the Grand Canal for half a century; his stories would fill ten novels, with interruptions for seating new arrivals, distributing menus and taking orders.

Here is his *plat du jour*:

"I'm about to snuff it, Raimondo," the Duke of N... said to me. "When you have closed my eyes, you must go down to the *campo*; you will sit down by the well; you will wait until a pretty woman goes by; I want her to be very, very pretty.... You will accost her civilly: 'Madame, the Duke, my master, has just yielded up his soul to God ... a few steps away from here.... His last wish: that a very pretty woman who was passing by should come and say a little prayer for him ... before he is taken away to San Michele...' "

"I did not have to wait long, Monsieur. A beautiful girl walks past, eighteen years old, with good firm breasts, just as the Duke liked. I go up to her. She hesitates. 'No one should disobey the wishes of a dead man, *signorina*.... *Povero!* The Duke said to me: 'One of my family, my brother, my sister-in-law, I don't mind.... A stranger would do the thing best'."

"She followed me. We went upstairs. The *letto matrimoniale*, the curtains drawn, the lamps.... The girl, tear drops in her eyes ... it was worth all the family's lamentations.... It was the Bygone face to face with Today. It was *il giorno vivente e la notte eterna*.

"When she was about to leave, I presented her with a little casket.... 'The Duke lived only for ladies; my master wanted his last thought to be for one of them. I have been asked to give you this...'

"In the casket, Monsieur, was an emerald worthy of the treasure in St Mark's, worthy of the *Pala d'Oro*."

1937

SHOULD VENICE be illuminated with neon lights? Those who look to the past say no; the futurists reply: "Despite what you say, St Mark's glistens in the light of our projectors; it's a great success; the tourists love it." The romantics hold firm; this morning they are parading on the square beneath a white banner: "WE WANT THE MOON."

1937

MILITARY PLANES bearing the lion of St Mark on their wings. After the sea, the sky. The future of dictators is in the sky, the Duce has said so.

A procession of little girls, hundreds of ribbons streaming from their shoulders; the *arditi* surround the well-booted townsfolk; their black, silken tassels gleam in the sunlight. It is the summoning of civilians, the *adunata* that takes place at five o'clock in the afternoon; avant-gardists and *balillas* take their places in squares marked out in chalk upon the ground of the *campi*, like pawns on a chessboard. Drivers stop in the middle of the Paduan countryside to don their black shirts before returning to Venice.

1937

ANCIENT INSCRIPTIONS were carved in stone; with their backs to the wall they confronted oblivion; they took eternity as their witness; they penetrated the heart of the countryside and were an integral part of the architecture; slight but immortal shadows, they kept pace with glory, victory or death. Nowadays, we no longer devote much time to the fact, we bring it about; we don't accredit the result, we call it up, we don't inscribe it, we just write it down, hurriedly, preferably on the least durable materials.

In Italy the Ethiopian war exacerbated that academic passion for combining inscriptions with *belles-lettres*. No one race has left behind more marks upon walls than the Latin people; they covered everything with them; on catacombs, barracks, circuses, in streets and alleyways you can still make out election announcements, mortgage deeds, appeals to some famous gladiator or renowned retiarius; Ovid and Propertius are quoted on the walls of Pompeii, between a couple of caricatures or lovers' dates; everywhere columns, tombs, aqueducts and statues still speak meaningfully to us over the centuries.

In our own time, one is scarcely past the Italian border than one is surprised to see that this remarkable dialogue between the State and its citizens continues. Who is it who writes? Who dictates? When did they cover the towns with the lapidary, heroic or familiar thoughts, which the Communists brought back into fashion here in about 1920?[22]

They are there, everywhere, those official phrases, daubed black on white, white on black. On the garage door of my hotel I read: *Fascism is an army on the march.* Above the municipal fountain: *Fascism is a global development.* At the entrance to the village: *Fascism is politeness.* The most current assertion is: *We shall be proved right*; and the death-head is seen everywhere, together with these simple words, which are hard to translate: *Me ne frego* (something like: *Who the hell cares* ... but more obscene).

The statements are most frequently aimed at Britain: *We shall not accept sanctions from anyone,* or: *British courtesy reeks of Abyssinian oil.* The slogan: *A noi, Duce*! defaces the most venerable of monuments, the walls of the Procuraties, stained grey by pigeon droppings, that old scraped bone that is Milan Cathedral, the sombre *palazzi* of Genoa and the mellow Signoria in Florence. And there's this one, which dates from the time of the call up: *Better to live the life of a lion for one day than live as a sheep for a hundred years*!

"Great poets need large audiences." No square, no esplanade, not even St Mark's would be able to contain the immense numbers of the public that Carlyle demanded. People stream past like water and the man in the street is obliged, however unwillingly, to listen to the strident, motionless cries that emanate from the walls of Venice, those talking walls of 1937. Of what interest are the bland affirmations, with their cold roman lettering, that are pasted up outside our town halls when compared to these exclamations? Their "no billstickers" doesn't frighten a soul.

The entire life of a country can be read either on the

front of houses, which for foreigners have become more instructive than a book, or at the rear, where they are transformed into notepads. It is readers who file past ideas, and not the reverse.

15 MAY 1938

AT THE NEWSPAPER KIOSK, Venice's *Il Gazzettino illustrato* is advertising an article entitled: "The Fatal Heroes". On the same page there is a photograph of Mussolini and Hitler at Stra. I buy the paper; the "fatal heroes": a series of historical pieces; the hero for that day: Byron.

1938
DEATH OF D'ANNUNZIO

IN THE 1930s, a friend had obtained an audience for me; summoned back to Paris, I had to cancel my visit to Gardone, and returned from Venice to France. On arrival at the fork on the motorway at Lake Garda, a fascist guard handed me a packet: "From the Comandante"; at that period French cars were not very numerous; he had picked out mine. Inside I found a paper-knife made of inlaid gold, bearing these words uttered by the national hero: "I only possess that which I give."

JUNE 1939

A T BLED, in Slovenia, by the lake shore, thirty kilometres from Ljubljana. An international tunnel is all
that separates two worlds, the Latin and the Slav, Julian
Veneto from Yugoslavia. One passes through fourteen
centuries in twenty minutes.

My wife is in Trieste, at her uncles' house. Mussolini
has just seized their Stock Exchange shares in order to
prepare for war, giving them in exchange state headed
notepaper and uncultivated land.

I was on my way to one of the Danube Commissions, two
hours away, for the spring session; a reduced Europe: the
Austrian admiral, a man of very noble blood and very tired;
the Romanian, our president, a wily and devious diplomat
on the brink of retirement; the Englishman, who drinks a
bottle of whisky a day—he died of it; the Yugoslav, petti-
fogging, blunt and loathed; the Italian, a buffoon.... Our
assignment: to supervise the Danube, both technically, and
a touch politically too, from Germany to the Black Sea.
Our winter session was held in March, in Nice; the autumn
one will take place in Galatz, at the mouth of the river, in
an old Second Empire—the age of Romania—palace that
is half-Turkish, half-Russian. Our old-fashioned yacht, flying the Commission's flag, along with those of eight
European nations, was berthed near Vienna. This very
peaceful Commission's only enemies were the rocks that
studded the Iron Gates, the silt which obstructed the fluvial
ports, or the fluctuations of the tributaries.

In this Slovenian countryside, that once formed the Austrian crown territories of Carinthia, Carniola and Styria, I was able to study at close quarters those Slavs who had been halted by the Alps on their march towards the Adriatic; they had rid themselves of Franz-Joseph's jurisdiction only to find themselves confronted by the Italians, who had grown rich on Austrian booty as a result of the 1920 treaties; the Italians had gained Trieste, Istria, Dalmatia and Julian Veneto; their mandate was to prevent the Slavs descending on the Adriatic; fascism took care of this, depriving Trieste of its hinterland, dena-tionalizing the towns, since they were unable to penetrate the countryside, dressing the Croats in black shirts and providing the Slovenes with boots.

With the end of the Serenissima, from 1814 onwards, Trieste, the Dominante, had prospered through the decline of Venice, which no longer needed to recruit slave oars-men for their galleys. Trieste, once made wealthy by Vienna, the Greeks, the English and the Germans, pros-pered little after 1920, deprived of the two-headed eagle, the city thought only of *italianità* and was indifferent to the miseries heaped upon priests and Slovenian teachers by the Irredentists, who purged the local administration and prohibited the Slav languages; after all, had not the Europe of the Treaty of Versailles been responsible for establishing the Italian presence, firstly in order to be rid of the Slavs, and then to contain them?

On the eve of war, these memories only served to remind one of the Slavs' tête-à-têtes with Venice; the Slavonians, the ancestors of those on the Riva degli Schiavoni, opposite the Danieli, where Victor-Emmanuel prances; coming down from Bled, approaching Trieste, I could hear them growling about their former masters; from high on the Dinaric Alps, the old lion of St Mark was living out the last days of its Adriatic splendour.

I would not see Venice again for another twelve years.

III

MORTE IN
MASCHERA

1950

Maria p..., a Venetian friend whom I questioned about the end of the last war, in which she herself had been involved, told me: "Venice was a dismal place during that winter of 1945; everything was rationed; news, especially: the local press was full of details about other fronts, about the German advance in Alsace, but was silent about what was taking place on our own doorstep; there were maps of the Neisse front, but nothing about the Ravenna-Bologna one. I could hear the bombs destroying Padua. There was no more electricity; the *vaporetti* had no fuel; there were notices on the walls providing descriptions of all sorts of lethal contraptions that fell out of the sky, which the public should not touch.

"On the 26th of April, my *Gazzettino* appeared in a smaller format. On the 27th of April, it had become a single sheet of paper: Milan occupied, Mussolini arrested, Canadian troops at Mestre. On the 28th, my newspaper was nothing but a leaflet, in which the Volunteers for Freedom and its glorious fighters were restoring the glory of the Risorgimento to Italy, which had been darkened by twenty years of Nazi-fascist barbarism. The Canadian armoured-cars would not stay for long; once Venice was taken, the Allies sped off in great haste: intent on preventing Tito from spilling over into the Julian Veneto...."

SEPTEMBER 1951

A EUROPEAN FESTIVAL, twenty years old today.... A
man of taste hurled his joy at being alive into the
Cannaregio. Did not Ludwig II of Bavaria drown himself
in two feet of water?

It would be absurd to talk about this latest evening like
a young girl discussing her first dance, but from the
moment I arrived I knew that I was coming to say farewell
to a certain world; a recluse through necessity and alone
these past eleven years, from the top of my glacier I suddenly fell upon a delightful skirmish, into a death knell of
the imagination. A ball? A ball in Italy, as in Stendhal!

In St Mark's Square, there was what a Venetian Montaigne would call "the throng of foreign peoples". It wasn't
a matter of hairdressers or make-up girls having missed
their trains or planes, of "ticket-holders" jeopardised by
last-minute defections—local politics, the American press,
left-wing puritanism and the resentment of those who had
been excluded were all blended together here.

On the terrace of Florian's, which was littered with
more feathers than an eiderdown, Churchill, his paint-
box in a shoulder-bag, held up his fingers in a V-sign, but
no one was interested; that day, V stood only for Venice.

Whether he was conscious of it or being challenging, it
was pleasing to think that a great amateur painter was
parading himself, just for the sake of bringing Venice back
to life, of helping those characters painted by great or lesser
masters—captive goddesses on their Gobelins tapestries,

who had grown bored on their museum canvases—to emerge from their frames; others could have done so, but only he dared; in a world of yellow-bellies, he was a *caballero*.

As I walked around, I admired a Venice that was inflamed in red and saffron, and I was reminded of spiny rock-fish, with monstrous heads, emerging from a dish of bouillabaisse.

We wanted to be the first, so that we could see without being seen. The porter examined our invitation cards as carefully as a cashier might look at a large denomination banknote, so many were the forged invitations circulating.

It was too early. B. was not yet dressed; he received us with good humour, his brow beaded in sweat, and in shirtsleeves, for he had not yet donned his Cagliostro costume, being more concerned with decorating his *palazzo*.

Leaning over the main balcony, which was festooned with girandole, I looked out over the spectators who had been squeezed into the narrow embankments and were hanging on to the cornices along the length of the houses. Only the church of San Geremia, lit tangentially like a backdrop in a theatre, separated the Palazzo Labia from the Grand Canal. In neighbouring windows, rented out for a fortune, heads were leaning out from stacked floors over the empty space below.

All that Venice could muster in the way of boats and small craft was compressed into this junction of the city's two biggest canals.

The windows of the *palazzi* were draped in tapestries, and the Aubusson carpets that ran down the steps were soaked in the waters of the Canal.

Through the exhaust fumes, the exhalations of tobacco and the smoke from the open-air rotisseries and burning torches, the projectors beamed down directly upon the first arrivals.

"*Miracolo vivente di sogno e poesia!*" cried a woman selling printed handkerchiefs beneath an open parasol, as she dashed off St Mark lions, one paw resting on the gospel.

Venice that evening added her own note of unreality to the illusions of a festival; the "guests" loomed out of the darkness into the *falso giorno* of a city that was herself a work of artifice. Lights concealed in corners beamed down as the caterpillar-like procession wended its way forward.

The theme of the spectacle: Marco Polo, the prodigal son, was returning home, bringing back with him to the Adriatic Chinese Chippendales or Turks painted by Liotard.[1]

Photographers from the world's press directed their gleaming lenses at the principal performers.

Between two figures of Barbary apes flanked by a Mandarin court, on Tartary junks more gilded than the *Bucintoro*, a Catalan with waxed moustaches basked in the beams of light. Damascened in silver, the giants followed. And behind them came the *goyescas*, their roles performed by descendants of Goya's models, who were given an ovation from the shops below to the roofs above.

The stream of fire that surged the length of these floating altars led towards the entrance to the Cannaregio, where those taking part in the procession set foot on a Savonnerie carpet drenched in the waters of the dark canal; upon disembarking, the women secured their footing with the help of Moorish porters who restored their delicate balance, flanked by two rows of yellow galley slaves, their oars held erect.

Chandeliers from Murano, decorated with real flowers, as delicate as those confections of threaded sugar that adorned Venetian festivals during the Renaissance, lit up the inner courtyard; there people were already bustling about preparing their tableaux vivants of the Beauvais tapestries that hung from the walls, the famous *Parties du monde*.

Without a care for the morrow, pleasure-loving Europeans, oil-rich Asians, bored Americans, kings from *Candide*, the jet-setters and a sea of shipowners continued to file past the church on the corner, where St Geremia did his best to restrain his lamentations: "You're heading straight for the cemetery…", he cried. "Watch out for San Michele!"

The masked apotheosis of that night twenty years ago was a Catherine II, a sky-blue sash across her bust, adorned, like some glacier, with diamonds from the Urals: she is no longer alive. I can see a Louis XIV in gold and white and, like some intoxicating perfume, I can still sniff his victorious presence; his sumptuous garb upset a colleague dressed in designer clothes, his hair as golden as a comet, who followed behind: today they are both dead. A Parisian Petronius who afterwards towered above the crowd of onlookers from the top of his palanquin, the very image of the glorious life, now sleeps in the peace of the graveyard. A bacchante, the English queen of Paris, dressed only in a panther skin, was led along by little Caribs; her steely eyes and her frosty laugh were extinguished forever immediately after her triumph.

Venice is the very last refuge on earth for the curious stroller; the free spectacle is a legacy from the Romans; everything offers the opportunity for amusement, the woman at her doorway whipping up mayonnaise, the Englishwoman at her easel, the solitary singer sitting on a gondoliers' bench, a child kicking his ball among the nibbling pigeons....

Leaving the Labia, the festival extended out on to the square. B...had wanted it to be so; in order to return to our hotel, in the direction of the station, we had to cross the Campo San Geremia; there everything danced, apart from the houses. Acrobats were reconstructing the famous pyramid, known as *The Strength of Hercules*, after the wooden model in the Correr Museum. The masked beauties had begun to mix with the crowd, who admired them without any envy; for the natural democracy of the Mediterranean people makes no distinction between the *piano nobile* and the pavement. (The first time I had observed this for myself was in the Appenines, at Vigoleno; the villagers had invaded the castle where Maria passed from the arms of her gardener into those of her chauffeur.)

Above our heads, a tight-rope walker dressed as a bear edged from one rooftop to another; tumblers and acrobats stood in pyramids, balancing at the level of the guttering; the prattle of the street salesmen and the jeers of the circus clowns drowned the splashing of the jousters on the canal and the shouts of the acrobats on their stilts.

Jean de Castellane, emerging from a ball at the Hôtel de Ville would mutter wearily: "It's like the street ... with a roof on top." In Venice, the street is like a *palazzo* without a roof.

It took twenty years for the Palazzo Labia, which was sold, to become a sad, peninsular administrative building.

Since these lines were written, the moving spirit of the resurgent Venice that evening has also passed on to the land of shadows.

After the tableaux vivants come the still-lifes.

1954

THE GIORGIONE EXHIBITION

GIORGIONE.... When I was twenty, people swore by him alone; Berenson and D'Annunzio had just discovered him. Everything was suddenly attributed to this genius who died very young; works by Titian, Cima de Conegliano, Sebastiano del Piombo, Palma the Elder and Lotto were seized and ascribed to this great unknown artist. My earliest savings were spent purchasing books by B.B. in which one unexpectedly discovered in Giorgione pre-Poussin landscapes, picturesque music, romanticism (*The Tempest*), the sensitivity of chiaroscuro, the Debussy-like atmosphere, created by shepherds with their theorbos, and the veils that Isadora Duncan wore; I remember a devout pilgrimage to Castelfranco (not daring to admit my disappointment at seeing his *Madonna*), in one of the earliest Fords....

Today it is the *Mostra* in Venice. In his introduction to the exhibition catalogue, Pietro Zampetti barely conceals his disillusionment. What remains of Giorgione? Three authentic portraits! What a battleground it's been! The critics can only agree about the *Pala* at Castelfranco, the *Three Philosophers* in Vienna and *The Tempest* from the Ospedale Civile; after one and a half centuries the *Judith* in Leningrad has been snatched by Raphael and restored to Giorgione for the time being, but doubts persist as to the *Young Man* in Berlin, the *Young Woman* in Vienna, the *Madonna* at the Ashmolean, the *Sleeping Venus* in Dresden, and the *Man with an Arrow* in Vienna. As for the *The*

Concert, there is talk of a collaboration with Titian…. The *Sick Man* may be by Leonardo. Even the *Three Ages* in the Pitti Palace are ascribed to Lotto; the most famous paintings by Giorgione are lost … others are attributed to the friend who shared his studio, Titian, with whom he had collaborated when they were pupils of Bellini's, and who, in his case, was lucky enough not to die at the age of thirty-three.

Everywhere, in Italian art criticism, one hears of nothing but *confusione* and *terreno di nebulosità*, of *influsso giorgionesco*, or *derivazione giorgionesca*. Giorgione is growing ever more distant….

Max Jacob

APRIL 1964

CRAZY BIDDING

ELEVEN O'CLOCK in the morning; it might have been dawn, the sky was so murky. This unwashed Venice reminds me of those postcards sent by Max Jacob, in which the cigar ash crushed into the gouache represented suburban fog. There was a biting north wind; we were walking along the Grand Canal, where the surface of the water was being pummelled by the wind, accompanied by the noise of those Italian motor engines that vibrate like a bowstring relieved of its arrow.

The auction began at midday, at the Palazzo Labia. Strapped tightly into his jacket, the forehead of an intellectual and slim as a sub-lieutenant, a precise, ingenuous look in his eye, a partaker of all the good things in life, M.R. had brought me along to the sale at the Labia, the last Venetian palace to disgorge its riches; he knew that all human possessions are nothing more than a warehouse....

Our munificent friend B. had decided to hold out against Time; to rebuild a palace was to reject the abyss, it was like writing the *Temps perdu*. Once his work was achieved, B. was no longer interested in it.

Even Proust, dreaming about what he would like to do once the Great War was over, imagined himself as the owner of a Venetian palace, where, "like Réjane", he would have invited the Poulet Quartet to play Fauré for him "as the dawn rose over the Grand Canal".

The frescoes in the *palazzo* were so famous in their day

185

that Reynolds and Fragonard made the journey to Venice in order to make copies of them. In the old days, at the turn of the century Labia, when the guide was showing people the paintings on the celebrated ceiling, he used to say: "*Signori*, PEGASUS PUTS CHRONOS TO FLIGHT."

Who will ever put Time to flight?

As we were walking along the canal, M.R. told me the history of the Labias: half a century of abusive power, of gold plates being hurled from the windows, of virgin walls being entrusted to the talents of Tiepolo, of Zugno, of Magno, of Diziani; ruined by Napoleon, the Labias had handed over the building to the Lobkowitz family, until a South African tycoon, who, extraordinarily enough, was also called Labia, bought back this house in which he wished he had been born. As they were negotiating the sale, he is said to have made the following play on words: *L'abbia o non l'abbia, sarò sempre Labia.*[2]

We had to clamber over barricades of paintings that looked even bigger now that they had been taken down, and over consoles, their gilt fading, which were being carried down the stairs as the rooms that had been laid waste by the auctioneers were cleared. Stripped of their chandeliers, the ceilings revealed rat holes and brickwork in a deplorable condition, its stucco chipped and flaking, held together by worm-infested pillars. Hollow footsteps echoed on the uncarpeted floors. Here, shorn of its former livery —Italian footmen trussed in gold like maritime proveditors—labourers were knocking back flasks of wine.

The Baroque, that exuberance of joy, cannot cope with neglect.

In the main courtyard, the international antique dealers, admired from a distance by the small traders from
the alleys of Venice, had taken their places. Experts and
dealers, who had flown in from Chelsea or Manhattan,
magnifying glasses in hand, were swamped by a stream of
noble effigies and horned doges, and mingled together
amidst a Capernaum of off-stage operatics. Tax inspec-
tors, Venetian fiscal authorities and spies from the Treasury
and Customs and Excise departments watched the future
bidders closely.

Beneath M. R.'s ivory hammer, an entire art-lover's
world would vanish; artefacts have no master.

Only the Tiepolos would remain, their fate bound to that
of the walls of the empty building: *The Negro with a Strawberry*,
The White Horse, *The Musicians' Gallery*, *The Embarkation of
Antony and Cleopatra*, *The Greyhound with Centurions*, the famous
perspective of *The Silver Dish*. Above them was the throng of
goddesses, painted as permanent frescoes, and who were
now mistresses of a deserted Palazzo Labia, laughing for all
eternity, like the Rhinemaidens.

Detached from their supports, in whose arms would
these beautiful women now lie? Where would these Bacch-
uses parade their drunkenness, or these Ceres their harvests? Casting a dark glance at their bidders, ermine-cloaked
doges on bituminous canvases no longer ascended the
Giants' staircase, but that of the auction house. Marshals
clutching their batons, ordered the assault, but the voices
of the auctioneers were louder. Removal men lolled about
on sinuous settees, intended for voluptuous siestas; light
from the chandeliers beamed down on the buyers; floating

upon this ocean of highly-valued objects were squadrons of Chinese vases, candelabra, girandola, jugs and pots. To the highest bidder for prows of ships that would never see battle again would go the coats of arms, destined for the hallways of Greek shipowners.

"At a hundred thousand lira, no further bids?"

Beneath the naked vaults, hewn from Istrian marble, the words echoed: No further bids....

These were the last rites for the life, not of a great collector, but of a great art lover ... Italy has one *camposanto* fewer....

1964

JUST AS IN 1917 I had observed Venice cast its shadow over my exiled life, similarly, as I left that auction sale, the Venice of the 1960s was to open up a gulf between my mature years and old age. Something, or someone, leads me, has always led me, whenever I believed I was paving my own path.

I look upon that world of yesteryear without resentment, nor regret; quite simply, it no longer exists; for me, at least, since it continues, without any bother or fuss, in a universe that is a little more brutal, a little more doomed, and in which the average level of virtues and vices must have remained more or less constant. It is merely that its ways are no longer mine; the barber cuts my hair with a pair of clippers; at the restaurant I am obliged to sit opposite my guest, not next to him, on a stool; hotels refuse my dog; when I arrive, the porter no longer takes the keys of my car in order to park it; at restaurants it is only in Greece that I am allowed to go and choose what I want from the stove; in Paris there is no longer any difference between the pavement and the road; at parties, I don't recognise people behind their beards and wigs, and I can't keep pace with so many first names. In the old days, the Mediterranean was my swimming-pool; nowadays, if I want to swim in it, I need the permission of the Russian or American fleets. Rheumatism confines me to drinking Vittel; can one go out in the evening without a glass in one's hand? It casts a chill on the evening and offends

189

one's hostess, who feels that her dinner party is thereby undermined. Paintings used to make me happy; today's art is the painting of iconoclasts. "You're a painter, why haven't you continued painting?" I asked Robert Bresson. "Because I would have committed suicide" he answered. As for dodecaphonic music, I only have to think of it to prefer death.

Awkward to look after, there's nothing left for me to do down here except make way; I shall never accustom myself to electronic gadgetry, nor to living in a country whose fate is being determined six thousand kilometres from where I live.

Everything sets one's teeth on edge in this world where it is always rush-hour and where children want to be Einsteins; the couples who go off to market clasping one another, as they see in the films, get on one's nerves; their kisses in public, it's no longer kissing, but eating; women's flesh is treated like meat. To crown it all, the young are far better looking than we were.

Yesterday, during mass in a little Canadian chapel, I was handed a cardboard box which everyone dipped into: it contained the hosts; as a child I was taught that to touch a host, even if it was not consecrated, was a sacrilege; I excused myself, saying that I could not take communion, not having been to confession in the morning; they smiled; it was quite customary to receive God without going to confession.

I have been away for too long; at home they speak a foreign language I no longer understand; besides, no dictionary exists.

Old age is governed by the minus sign: one is less and less intelligent, less and less foolish.

Autumn; lying fallow until now, the dead leaves begin to stir, clinging to the rim, rolling on towards winter.

1963

SERENATA A TRE 196…

THIS PIAZZETTA reminds me of something…. An earlier disappointment, some misadventure that lay dormant here, unperturbed by memory for years … I allude to it only because after such a long time it seems to me to take on a symbolic value.

Cats in Venice never disturb themselves either, having nothing to fear from cars; the only criticism I have of cats is that they never say good morning. Venetian cats look as if they are a part of the ground; they don't wear collars; their bellies are like deflated bagpipes, and in this treeless city they no longer know how to climb; they are weary of life, for there are too many mice, too many pigeons.

Here is one of them, painted on the outside of this little house. I am reminded of Tintoretto and of Giorgione, who both began life as house painters …

Here I am … so many years ago …

Beguiling C…. Even her ghost makes a fool of me! Who would not be led astray, beyond the grave? When she enraptured me, C… certainly did not corrupt my innocence, but how often did I leave her, raging at the confusion she brought to my emotions; and I was even more furious when her reappearance was enough to crush all resentment.

How to explain it? That insolent way she held her head, her enigmatic eyes, defiant and yellow as the deepest agate, her nose with its quivering nostrils, her unruly hair that was like a fire no hat could extinguish. The centuries blended in her, she was proud like the Renaissance, as frivolous as the Baroque. A queen and a rag-and-bone woman; a sibyl and a little girl.

She travelled throughout her life, even within Venice, staying one year with aristocrats, another living among the women who threaded pearls or the boatmen on the Giudecca. She, who never opened a book, where did she gain a general knowledge that was often erudite? The key to that beautiful, fleshly enigma is not one to be unlocked easily.

She was so delectable that her mere presence was a veritable assault on one's morals. Very tall, she would examine you thoroughly and with expertise from on high; you felt that even if you lay her on her back she would still pinch you, like a crab, that she would never ask for mercy, always consenting, but never giving of herself.

That was what I was suddenly reminded of by the little house in the Piazzetta, and the cat painted *a tempera* on the cartouche.

"Come this evening, after dinner.… Don't come in by the door to the canal, you'd be seen too easily. Go by the back door, the *campo* is always deserted."

That evening, the door was ajar. The drawing-room was empty.…

If she had changed her mind, C… would not have left the house unlocked; she would be expecting me, hoping that I would come, she would keep our appointment. I went straight to the bedroom, like a gourmand drawn to the kitchen. The door was unbolted.

"C…, it's me!"

I could smell her behind the door.

I looked through the key-hole; a shirt was in the way. C… liked playing pranks, and I also knew she was a tease. But why leave me still yearning?

My ear at the door-frame, my hands on the cold marble mantel-piece. I hold my breath: there are two women. I can hear them satisfying one another; the pleasures of the eavesdropper; that lapping sound is not water splashing against the door of the house … I was granted the entire sequence, right up to the squealing of a rabbit carried away by rapaciousness….

Afterwards there was silence, total suspense. I knocked, hoping that it was just a curtain-raiser, C… was someone who liked to share. Nothing.

Every minute made me feel more foolish, more lonely, more excluded.

That evening, to my great disappointment, the door was not opened; everywhere Industry prevailed over Labour….

I never knew the secret of that evening. Later on, I heard tell of a family story, involving two female cousins. Who had insisted on that door being shut? C…, out of malice? The other person, out of jealousy or prudery, or because she liked secrecy? Or was it Man, in the person of myself, being pilloried?

Both of them are dead; they moan elsewhere, stoking the fires of hell. Above the entrance to the little house, I find the cartouche on the distempered wall: there one sees a cat lusting after two smoked herring….

I returned to the hotel, blaming myself and meditating bitterly on the role of men today, poor subjugated

194

conquerors, routed by the feminist triumph that is breaking out everywhere; governors governed; one-time masters
of the house doing the shopping, like Jouhandeau,[3] whose
slavery is the explanation for his wonderful portraits of Élise
(like all men, Marcel is a coward; what redeems him is that
at the last moment he reveals himself, through his sensitivity, to be more of a woman than women themselves…).

We are seeing the dawn of a primitive matriarchy, a
post-nuclear one, it occurs to me. The despotic Don
Juans and pimps, revealed to us in their majesty in so
many cliché-ridden accounts, are nothing but poor sub-
missive little girls who have surrendered. The recent
strike by women in the USA, the republishing of *Lysistrata*;
democracy, the blackmailer of the weak, brackets the
Female with those who were once subjugated, the Blacks,
servants, the working class, children and all those liber-
ated people who have become the masters. The compo-
sition of the masses will change, but the masses will
remain; that is what is meant by "revolution", the ety-
mology indicates the nature of the word: a return to the
point of departure. Women, for their part, will recover
from all this and will perfect their sensual aspirations. I
can remember those handsome Berber farmers, who had
come down from the Rif mountains and were being
forcibly led to the souks by their wives; I used to come
across them in Tangiers, being coaxed along by them
into the shops and spending a fortune on useless necklaces, gaudy silks and hideous furnishing materials; once
they were back home, they left all their fine apparel on
their doorsteps and went back to their labours.

SEPTEMBER 1965
FROM THE TOP OF THE
CAMPANILE

Fʀᴏᴍ ᴛʜᴇ ᴛᴏᴘ of the Campanile I survey the whole of
Venice, which is as spread out as New York is vertical, as salmon-pink as London is black and gold. The
whole place is bathed in showers, very much like a watercolour, with off-whites and dull beiges, picked out by the
dark crimson shades of walls that look like the flesh of
tuna. A violent breeze ripples through the Lagoon, driving clouds that are as light as those new nylon sails at the
regattas on the Lido.

Through the iron bars on the top floor, which dissuade
those contemplating suicide from doing so, I could see St
Mark's as if glued to the Doges' Palace, at once a refuge,
a treasury and an exit door from one of the wings of the
theatre that is Venice. From this platform, one understands better the true role of St Mark's, which was that of
a private chapel to the Palace, not a public building as it
is today, and not a basilica as is commonly believed.

At the entrance, I could make out the four figures on the
porphyry relief with their broken boxer's noses; the four
Lysippus horses were leaping into the clouds, Venice's only
horses bowing their necks to which the gold still adheres,
proud to be on view, but regretting, as former champions,
that they could not challenge Colleone's mount, or, if need
be, Victor-Emmanuel's prancing palfrey.

Perhaps the St Mark's horses were nostalgic for their

journey to Paris in 1798, their farewell to the tearful
Venetians, their walk to the quayside and their embarkation aboard the French frigate *La Sensible*, their arrival at
Toulon amidst all the paintings from the Italian campaign, their apotheosis on the Champ-de-Mars, behind
the dromedaries and their installation on the Arc du
Carrousel, to the accompaniment of formal addresses:

Et si de tes palais ils décorent le faîte
C'est par droit de vertu, non par droit de conquête.[4]

Anchored in front of San Giorgio Maggiore, the bulk of
a British aircraft-carrier distorted the proportions, concealing the Lido which lay on the horizon, like a sleeping
crocodile on the surface of the water. From on high I
scanned the play of the currents, varying in shade according to the salt content, where the antique green intersected the dirty green, the colour of excavated jade.
Waterways marked out with stakes that are sunk into the
mud, and slumbering dykes through which only the pilots
and the old fishermen know how to find their way.

Goethe and Taine have described this view, from this
very point; they saw those tables from Quadri's café dot-
ted in front of the Procuraties. Up there, I thought of
Byron's remark: "Nature alone does not lie", ... except
for Venice, which does make nature lie and surpasses her;
only man has dared put this challenge to the physical and
architectural laws; what other creature—apart from the
swallow building its nest—can make a soft substance
hard? Who would have dared slosh about in this mud?

"The object is never as dark as its reflection", painters

say; only the reflection of Venice in our memories is lighter than the reality.

Who would attempt to build her again?

1965

Discovered in Cassini's bookshop in the Via 22 Marzo the *Memoirs* of the last Doge, Ludovico Manin: "10 May 1797; the French are at Mestre, any resistance is useless; the Serenissima arranged to bring in Dalmatian troops, but not in sufficient number. Without any bounty, Venice runs the risk of pillaging and fire." "Tonight," adds the doge, "we shall not sleep in our beds." Poor Manin, whose graphic coat of arms bore an Adonis asleep beneath a tree....

The Council of Ten decided to let the consul, Villetard, know that the government of Venice would welcome the French troops "in a friendly manner". The words over-did it; let the Venetians keep their friendship for them-selves, Villetard replied to the Doge.

On the 12th of May, the Slavic troops re-embarked for Dalmatia from the Giudecca. The French arrived. Would it mean a bloodbath? No. Manin shed tears as nobody has shed them since Diderot. Seven days later, there was a masked ball at the Fenice; both French and Venetian guards at the doors. On the 22nd, a *Te Deum* at St Mark's. Contributions to the war were raised; hostages; the *Libro d'oro delle nobiltà veneziana* was burnt. Another party at the Fenice, not very successful; how was it possible not to be frightened when you knew that Bonaparte, a few leagues away from here, had exclaimed: "I shall be the Attila Venice"?...[5] General Baraguay, who was staying at Palazzo Pisani, held a reception; co-operation was *languida*.

A committee from the Directoire arrived and searched through the libraries, taking away five hundred rare books and manuscripts and thirty of the best paintings.

On the 14th of August, Masséna moved into the Palazzo Gradenigo. Families that owned more than one gondola had to relinquish them to the occupying forces, together with the gondoliers, who were expected to provide food for themselves; the conscripts fled. Nevertheless, five theatres remained open. Sérurier arrived, with a large general staff; the Arsenal was emptied; they set fire to the *Bucintoro*. The end of the Serenissima (*Memoirs* of L. Manin, Venice, 1886).

Mallet du Pan, at the time, Molmenti, later on, and Guy Dumas in our own time, have persuaded us that Venice was corrupt and ridden with vice; she was no more so than the rest of Europe, this Serenissima that had endured for thirteen centuries, and whose disappearance was lamented by all her people.

Whether it was 1797 or 1945, any more the soldiers of the Directoire than the New Zealand armoured car troops under the command of the English General Freyberg, Venice has scarcely put up fierce resistance; she wanted to avoid pillage and fire; the names of the conquering generals are forgotten in a few months, treaties turn yellow after ten years, and empires will never be other than empires; the duty of a unique city is to survive.[6]

APRIL 196...

THE HEIGHTS and the depths of Venice, where human life fluctuated for so long between two extremes, between *piombi* and *pozzi*, between the drains up above, and the wells beneath; a town of poor fishermen and a golden city; along the same canal passed both the Wagner of the duet from *Tristan* and the man of the funebral gondola, his own. *Non nobis, Domine....*

1908–1970

THE THREE AGES OF MAN

How many years, social circles, fashions, pledges and hopes have I seen pass by beneath these Procuraties, among these after-dinner strollers.... The soldiers from the time of the Triple Alliance carrying their sabres that were never drawn, under their arms; their bulging riding britches and their loose-fitting boots, Tor di Quinto style, with wide regimental stripes, yellow, blue and cerise, and their huge kepis and their plumes, wearing a monocle and a curled-up Wilhelm II moustache; the Venetian women in their black shawls (and the noise of their clogs on the pavement, now nothing but a memory); the beautiful foreign women, with their feathered boas and their high collars drawn taut with stays, holding their dress in one hand, a tortoise-shell lorgnette or a fan in the other.

Next came the Allied armies in their green and bronze, or khaki uniforms, and their medals.

Then the blackshirts, the Balbo-like beards, the riding britches once more, but this time worn down to the knees, in the knickerbocker style, like the Guards; and still those boots, now very tight-fitting; the rhythmic march, the banners, the stacks of weapons and the commemorative crowns, followed by the ministers in gaiters (in morning coats and bowler hats); more ladies, sportswomen wearing eye-shades in the style of Suzanne Lenglen, or *balillas*.... Workers' marches.... In about 1935, the Mussolini style gave way to uniforms in the Hitler mould: white tunics over tobacco-coloured trousers.

Pursuing History at a trot, it is now the Liberation, with American jackets everywhere and high-laced military boots; armbands bearing the letters MP, cowboy shirts and open collars, Kodak cameras with telephoto lens, and Lucky Strikes in their holsters.

And now here we are today: weeping willow hairstyles, bell-bottoms worn over oilskins, dresses cut from old curtains that drag along among the rubbish, sandals, bare feet, a sleeping-bag over the shoulder, the pilgrimages to the source. It's a time of letting go, of "let's crash down here, no point in going any further".

I shall bring this procession of ghosts through St Mark's Square to a halt, not being a Carpaccio; nor a Saint-Simon, who nevertheless wrote: "These trifles are scarcely ever included in the *Memoirs*; however, they give an accurate idea of almost everything one looks for in them."

There's a dispute between the Venice city council and the military authorities which, like their equivalents in every country, do not want to relinquish anything. Venice is still scattered with islands or islets which are no loger of any strategic importance: Santo Spirito, Lazaretto Vecchio, La Celestia, San Giacomo in Palude, La Certosa…. Those old monasteries, those fortresses that have nothing to defend…. The Italian empire is long past and the Office of Tourism requires hotels and more hotels.

PIAZZALE ROMA
197...

WHAT THE railway line began, the pneumatic tyre has achieved. The land takes it revenge over the sea; ever since 1931 those who supported terra firma were the victors, having their way against Mussolini who, being artistically minded, wanted to cut off Venice from the Italian mainland.

Confronted with a garage for mammoths, Europe hurls herself upon Venice, hurriedly devours her, and then goes away again. Thieves who steal spare wheels, those who falsify police placards, money-changers, hitch-hiking prostitutes and other knaves add to the confusion of the pilgrims in a Europe that is trying to patch together her different parts.

Bridges built of ancient brick are interspersed with footbridges made of concrete, which are themselves over-looked by the multi-lane flyovers. The eurobuses and trains on rubber wheels holding eighty passengers pass minibuses setting off for Nepal. The whole of this Santa Croce district smokes with gas and carbon monoxide, Cinzano fumes and marijuana. Collapsing suitcases that have fallen off the top decks of buses like moraines from a moving glacier, the Japanese with their top-heavy Leicas, the 16mm film strewn over the ground, the mattresses and rolled-up sleeping-bags, bulging more with cooking utensils than with stuffing, everybody converges in this hotchpotch of humanity where people who have driven through the night try to glimpse Venice on a morning such as this, when the sun has not managed to pierce through the kilometres of dust.

Unlike the Basilica of St Mark's, the Piazzale Roma is a cathedral of drivers. You have to choose between the museum and life.

IV

IT'S EASIER TO START THAN IT IS TO END

AT THE DOGES' PALACE
23 SEPTEMBER 1967

WHO WOULD ATTEMPT to build Venice again? One man ventured to do so, Volpi, in full flight, in October 1917, *anno fra i più tristi della storia d'Italia*. On land that one would hardly dare call firm, he constructed Italy's second port, Porto Marghera, in a terrain that bred malaria, mosquitoes and frogs. It developed into two thousand solid hectares of refineries and factories producing aluminium or refined nitrogen.

In a few days' time we shall celebrate the fiftieth anniversary of this astonishing enterprise; in this very place, at the Doges' Palace, the first Venice is to pay homage to the founder of the second, *il signor conte Volpi di Misurata*.

Having climbed the Giants' Staircase, then the Scala d'Oro, I enter the Great Council room, and I stand beside the woman who was the constant and kindly shadow of the celebrated Venetian.

Seventy-two doges look down upon us, lined up between the victories won by la Serenissima that are painted on the walls. Facing one another are the Gothic bays giving on to San Giorgio Maggiore, bathed in the setting sun, and Tintoretto's *Paradise*. Above our heads, as if sculpted from a massive piece of gold, the immense oval of the ceiling painted by Veronese pierces the joists that seem to be pushed upwards by the brushwork of the clouds towards a sky that is higher than the actual one; the structural details disappear beneath the golden profusion of this floating *Bucentaurus*.

The last time I had seen Volpi was in Paris, in his hotel bedroom, in 1943; I discovered a man who was worn out by events, and whose gigantic creation was being called into question from the Adriatic to Libya; within a quarter of a century everything had been lost. I thought again about what Philippe Berthelot had frequently told me, by way of justifying the long anti-Italian tradition of the Quai d'Orsay: "They're a mediocre instrument, we shall never do anything with the Italians." (That's true of war, which is Death, but it's not true of industry, buildings, agriculture, which are Life.)

The Venetians are made of stern stuff and are proof against the deluge. They always extricate themselves; their houses all have two exits, one on the water, the other on land.

A victory in Venice is worth a hundred victories anywhere else.

Tonight is very much a final victory for Volpi the Venetian. The whole of Venice is here: the Cardinal Patriarch brings the Pope's blessing; Andreotti, that of the government; he reads a telegram from Saragat celebrating the "genius of the man"; the Under-Secretary of State to the Treasury pays tribute to someone who, as Mussolini's Minister of Finance, and with the backing of the Bank of England and loans from Morgan, saved his country; the Syndic and the whole Municipality of Venice listen to an account of Volpi's life over many reigns, not one of which witnessed an undertaking that could not be ruined: what Volpi wanted, fifty years ago, exists; the 100,000-ton and more oil tankers enter by Malamocco and arrive at Mestre. At home, nobody would mention his name; here, they think only of the glory of the very serene Serenissima; politics are forgotten; we are among Venetians; Italy is but one century old, Venice fifteen, and the old adage remains true: *Veneziani, poi Cristiani*! (Venetians first, then Christians).

OCTOBER 1970

YESTERDAY I WAS at the Venice Courthouse. A photographer from Chioggia was being tried, accused of holding arty parties, which were attended by young Venetian boys. Alerted by the number of cars with Treviso, Padua and Trieste numberplates that were being parked there at night, the Chioggia police burst into his studio; the guests fled through the windows. The man's lawyer pleaded not guilty, Merlin's law on prostitution not being applicable, according to him, to male prostitution.

8 OCTOBER 1970

At the Fenice, the first performance of Aretino's *Cortigiana*, by the Teatro stabile, at the "Festival of Prose". Two parallel "witticisms": a man from Siena, a candidate for the cardinalate, is learning the art of becoming a courtier; he is brought on in a curious piece of machinery, a sort of oven for shaping courtiers; an amorous Neapolitan braggart (*gran vantatore*) arrives; a procuress, who is meant to smooth his path, substitutes the baker's wife for the woman he idolizes. There were a great many secondary characters, the most successful being the caricature of a man of letters, attired in manuscripts, the pages of which were sewn on to his costume and hung down, making him look like a bookstall.

The performance was "perishingly" boring, as Lucien Daudet used to say. Dialogue in regional dialect, obscene allusions and anti-clericalism in the worst possible taste: "Here come the Turks! For fear of being impaled, everyone has fled, apart from the priests"; incomprehensible and ignorant comments on literature or contemporary politics. The actors declaimed for five acts, *abusando del registro urlato*; dramatic art nowadays consists of nothing but exaggerated and bawled-out aggression; actors, whose job it is to "look as though" they are doing something, ought to be taught that they should look as if they are shouting, without actually doing so. If only they would give us Aristophanes, Calderón or Shakespeare, instead of constant Brecht. The result was the following, from

213

this morning's *Corriere*: "The audience, which to begin with was very large, disappeared during the interval." "*Il pubblico, molto numeroso all'inizio, ha calato durante l'intervallo.*"

AUGUST 1969

THIS EXTREMITY of the Adriatic is a real lobster pot ... All the refugees throughout History; within the arms of her lagoons the sea cradles a never-ending *exodus*: confronted with swamps that are impassable, Goths, Avars, Lombards have had to relinquish their prey; it was here that Philip-Augustus watched the Jews slip through his fingers, and where the Pope gave up trying to track down Aretino. Today, it is still Venice, rather than Crete and Istanbul, that the hippies, those scavengers after the Absolute, opt for before they set off from "foul" Europe.

I was coming out of one of those little delicatessens that are hidden away behind the Danieli, among the narrow streets at right angles to the quayside, where bedrooms as big as trunks can be rented by the day. Beneath the span of the Bridge of Sighs my eyes were dazzled by the setting sun which had transformed the entrance to the Giudecca, to the west of San Giorgio Maggiore, into a pool of rose essence.

I had just caught a whiff of a stench of goat: I was to leeward of three young men whose bare torsos had been scorched in the furnaces of the travelling life; they wore gold crosses around their necks, naturally. Their beauty was more offensive than ugliness. A protesting Valkyrie, her hair spread across shoulders gnawed by salt, appeared to be keeping them on a tight rein, reminiscent of some stone-age matriarchy; their armpits smelt of leeks, their buttocks of venison; their sleeping-bags rolled beneath their necks, they

215

were stretched out, looking as if they had been shot, on the floor of a money-changer's shop, against a background of international gold coins. They had let themselves go to such a degree that they seemed to have forgotten how to use chairs and they squatted down nimbly and naturally. Their fingers, the colour of iodine, rolled forbidden cigarettes; the chewing gum in the mouth of the third of them, an American, incorporated the national pastime of masti-cating with a naturally bovine brutishness. What could possibly restrain these creatures: some Bonaparte who had mistaken the century, a Chateaubriand who would never write a word, a Guatamelata without a destiny, a Lope de Vega without a manuscript? To imagine them at the age of eighty sent a shiver down the spine.

I came across them again on my way back from the Lido the following evening, seated Buddha-like with their life-belts on, at the back of a *vaporetto*; these spineless young things did not know how to stand vertically.

We were approaching the Giardini. As we coasted along, the vapours ripped through the lagoon like scissors cutting through a length of silk; the water was frothy and whipped up with dirty snow like a real *cappuccino*.

I handed the Valkyrie my flask of grappa; the wretched ragamuffin grabbed it without a word of thanks.

"Man can revert to being an ape or a wolf in six months," I launched forth, "but to produce a Plato, it must have taken millions of years.… As for conceiving of Venice…"

"I shit on Venice," replied the Valkyrie.

"You can leave that to the pigeons, Mademoiselle…" I said, taking back my empty flask.

1969

VENICE IN THE AUTUMN, disinfected of tourists (apart from the unbudgeable Buddha-like hippies, so lacking in any curiosity), her buildings decked in dust covers, cloaked in rain; it's the least frivolous time. Venice in spring, when her paving stones start to sweat and the Campanile is reflected in the lake that forms in St Mark's Square. Venice in winter, the time of the *temperatura rigida* and the *congelamento*, when the fire-wardens watch out for fires in the tall chimneys, and the wolves come down from the Dolomites. As for Venice in summertime, it's the worst time....

1970

A N OVERCAST October sky this morning; an opaline grey, the colour of old chandeliers, so fragile that they sell marabou feathers with which to dust them.

1970

O N THIS OCTOBER EVENING, it was still summertime; the surface of the water was like a piece of shattered glass, with tug-boats wailing, transporter bridges scattering the flocks of seagulls that rested on the mud-flats, pilot ships towing sea-going oil tankers, ferries from the Lido disgorging their vehicles from both ends, and motor boats constructed of nickel, chrome and mahogany clattering against a surface hardened by speed; they are driven by elegant bare-chested Tritons who steer standing up—they are ashamed to steer sitting down in Venice. Everything seemed to be churning up the brackish water and to be drawing it towards itself as one might a sheet; this water disappeared beneath the hulls, just as in those regattas painted by Guardi in which the scores of gondolas transform the Grand Canal into a pontoon bridge.

THE SAME DAY

Venice … rather than being a seminary of *morbidezza* is an academy of energy; Barrès might have been able to draw strength here by touching the water rather than the earth. That evening Venice-the-Red, where, in Alfred de Musset's time, not a boat stirred, could offer nothing but deafening sirens, whipped up waves and a sky perforated by jet planes; everywhere lights burned brightly, people shouted and everything was steaming with perspiration.

As we drew up in front of the Danieli, night was falling, but the constant hubbub continued; the flecks of froth clung to the bows until we reached the steps of the jetty. This screech of outboard motors wailing at five thousand revolutions per minute and the traffic pounding by all served to mount a challenge to that old literary hack whom we call Death; everything seemed to cry out: "Enough debris, enough relics, enough remains, put a stop to all this twilight! Enough of this moaning from such a gay city!"

In the old surroundings, life went on, rather like a play by Beckett performed in the amphitheatre at Nîmes.

Venice became once more what she had been in the fifteenth century, a sort of Manhattan, a predatory city of extremes, howling with prosperity, with a Rialto which had been the Brooklyn Bridge of its age, and a Grand Canal that was a sort of Fifth Avenue for millionnaire doges; her airfields recalled the fleets of galleys sponsored by bankers; an Italian city without any Italians, like New York without Americans, where the Blacks, in this case, were fair-haired

Dalmatians, and the Jewish brokers Greek shipowners (for, in the vicinity of San Giorgio dei Greci, the Greeks, who had come from Rhodes and Chios after the fall of Constantinople, were the true monarchs of the Republic, and her most famous courtesans were Greek too).

Throughout History, Venice has shown two faces: sometimes a pond, sometimes the open sea, one moment peddling lethargy in bookshop windows, the next exploding into a far-flung imperialism (one that was so despotic that Christian Levant, weary of her harshness, came to prefer the Turk).

Venice will be saved; offices installed in the Palazzo Papadopoli, run by scholars from every nation, are dedicated to doing so: a Californian oceanographer, an expert in smoke pollution, has flown in from Los Angeles; a specialist in terrestrial sub-stratas from Massachusetts, and another, an earthquake engineer from the Soviet Union; it's called the Bureau for the Study of Maritime and Terrestrial Movement. Venice's fate lies in the hands of these men. Based on information received from computers, their great project is to close the three entrances to the lagoon with gigantic air balloons that can be inflated or deflated at will.

Due to the proximity of the two shores, tides in the Adriatic are much more violent and unpredictable that those in the rest of the Mediterranean; storms blow up as if inside a shell. (I was once nearly ship-wrecked, off Ancona, in 1920.)

Venice is sinking thirty centimetres every century, which is not much more than the rest of the world, but

Porto Marghera and Mestre, by pumping out excessive amounts of water, have destroyed the natural balance of the lagoon.

SEPTEMBER 1970

A FASCINATING EXHIBITION at the Palazzo Grassi: "The History of the Venetian Lagoon"; the geology, hydrography, botany, the navigation, the Gondola through the ages; hunting, fishing, the Lagoon in Literature and History. There were excellent ten foot-long maps on parchment: one by Ottavio Fabri and Sabbadino, from the sixteenth century; another by Minorelli and Vestri from the seventeenth. A Venetian mosaic of the Flood, dating from 589. Some xylographs depicting the construction of a twelfth century Venice; no machinery, no dredger, nothing but human labour; wooden stakes are being dug in by hand by two workmen lifting wooden mallets; it really was the republic of beavers of which Goethe spoke.

And what a surface! There are examples here of the silt, of reeds used for the first fences, of lichen hanging from some nameless mush.

Sometimes I attempt to drain the lifeblood out of myself by imagining Venice dying before I do, imagining her being swallowed up without revealing her features upon the water before she disappears. Being submerged not to the depths, but a few feet beneath the water; her cone-shaped chimneys would emerge, her miradors, from which the fishermen would cast their lines, and her campanile, a refuge for the last cats from St Mark's. The *vaporetti*, tilting under the weight of visitors, would survey the surface of the waters where they coalesce with the mire of the past; tourists would point out to each other the gold from some mosaic, held afloat by five water-polo balls: the domes of St Mark's; the Salute would be used as a mooring buoy by cargo ships; bubbles would float up from above the Grand Canal, released by frogmen groping around for American ladies' jewels in the cellars of a submerged Grand Hotel. "What prophecy has ever turned a people away from sin?" said Jeremiah.

Venice is drowning; it may well be the best thing that could happen to her.

IN CRETE
CANDIA (HERAKLION)
APRIL 1970

O NE IS STILL in Venice, here, on the square where the lions on the Morosoni fountain belch forth from their mouths the melted snow from Mount Ida upon the citizens of Heraklion. It is a Venice that is far removed from the dreaded gusts of the bora, a Venice for the end of winter. On the square, the tables and chairs from the café spill out over the pavement and on to the road; I watch the passers-by; a bearded pope upon a puny donkey, people selling foreign newspapers that arrived on the midday plane, elderly peasants, still dressed in the Turkish clothes that were worn before the revolution, with a black turban wrapped around their grey heads, baggy trousers and scarlet boots made from goatskin.

Venice is returning to Greece what she stole from her; for more than four centuries she protected Crete, especially this town of Candia, which was besieged by the Turks for twenty-three years. This morning, I climbed the ramparts and clambered up on to the old red-brick parapets with their imitation fortifications, that first line of walls, built at the foot of Foscarini's breaches, from which the scree crumbled, carrying down with it the jumble of centuries in an avalanche of stones emblazoned with the coat of arms of la Serenissima, Roman sarcophagi and curtains worn away with age.

El Greco left for the city of Toledo just in time, but

Candia, confronted with Islam, stood firm. In those days, the white race was not ashamed of its hegemony, or of its Duke of Crete, who was appointed by the Adriatic doge; it scoffed at the wrath of Ahmet, the grand vizier who burned his prisoners alive. La Feuillade and the Duc de Beaufort (the "roi des Halles", and natural son of Henri IV), and the Hanoverian or Bohemian conscripts died here, for the West, adding their bodies to the ramparts built by San Micheli, the Venetian architect.

At dawn, facing the old port, the still sea beneath the sun-shades, a scene from a Claude Lorrain greeted me upon waking; everything was there, the vaulted docks that had been dug to house the old Venetian galleys, the crenellated battlements along the winding road, the black, tarred fishing-nets laid out in half-circles, the lateen sails with their oblique initials that impede the background view of the barbicans and casemates that had been demolished by earthquakes. The surface of the sluggish waters had not yet been scored by any propeller, or carressed by any oar; only an underwater swimmer's flippers appeared between the breakwaters, like the dorsal fin of some submerged monster.

Venice had handed over her authority to other imperial powers; would the most recent of these, whose net was cast from Odessa to Mers el-Kébir, last longer than that of the Carthaginians, the Romans, the Normans, Byzantium, the Turk, or the British? The Venetian empire is still alive in Crete; here, she still holds sway; she is the "great presence" that the *Italienische Reise* talk about. It is as if Venice had never been expelled from the Orient; the day that Christopher Columbus discovered America was when la Serenissima chose to let herself expire; Vasco da Gama, by rounding the Cape of Good Hope, delivered the fatal knot; she survived for no more than three centuries, which is a great deal when one thinks that it only took a mere twenty years for the British Empire to become but a shadow of itself.

At midday I entered the bazaar, which was ablaze with oranges and lemons spilling from their baskets, peppers the colour of the Spanish flag, and kid goats with their throats slit. Between the arsenal and the cemetery the shops were parading their right to life, stretching out their medieval awnings, which were doing their best to support the overhanging moucharabies built of grey sycamore wood, dating from before Independence.

Gathered together around a glass of water outside the bars, with their bulging stalls and the cafés whose floors were pink with the dissected prawns consumed with apéritifs, were a dozen or so notable Cretans; the cheap restaurants hissed with the smoke from the frying. Clusters of hippies, perpetual castaways on the raft of leisure, drooled at the sight of cauldrons full to overflowing with snails cooked in onions, of grills upon which meatballs with lemon, or *giouvarlakia*, steamed alongside *mizithra*, cheeses made from honey, piled up in stacks.

In front of the Takio taverna, an English minibus, looking like a prehistoric cavern on Dunlop tyres, had given up the ghost; the foul stench of a public rubbish dump seeped from the open door, through which could be seen the remnants of gnawed bones on aluminium plates that had been placed on jerrycans; from the roof hung used espadrilles and plastic bags. A smell of pork in wine-flavoured sauce had enticed out of the vehicle a group of Nordic creatures, whose skin had turned to leather, and whose dark glasses were attempting to make a home for themselves in the fur-covered faces from which the only thing to emerge was an aubergine-coloured nose. In the winter the hippies had covered their naked torsos with a sheepskin bought from some shepherd or other on Mount Ida. I recognized these famished creatures: they were my English friends and my Yankee with the structuralist beard, the ones I had come across last summer in Venice. Exhausted by all the spare time they had on their hands, the little band were examining their pocket money, scrutinizing the menu in Greek and consulting one another, torn between the desire to eat something other than stolen chickens and the threat of arrest, followed by repatriation by the British consulate. (The Orthodox Church is not as indulgent towards vagabonds as the Roman Church.) Painted in white on the sides and on the back of their minibus, in three languages, were the words:

THE BOURGEOISIE STINKS

"A conventional fellow invites you to have some lunch," I told them.

What would be the use of achieving my grand old age if one did not feel closer to a tramp outdoors in Crete eating two-drachmas' worth of spaghetti from a paper plate, than to a conventional French family sitting at table in front of a haunch of venison braised in port wine?

I often feel jealous of lovers of the open road; they provide substance for a whole variety of dreams that Balzac described as: "the life of a Mohican", and they remind me of our own life in 1920, of the way we heaped insults on society, our need for destruction and our defiant challenges scrawled on posters at the time that the Treaty of Versailles was bleeding Europe to death; they make me relive our attitude of "to hell with everyone", "to blazes with everything". But as for this lot, what will they do when they have finished wandering along the verges of non-existence? I make fun of them, I feel sorry for them, I envy them.

I asked them about how they spent their time: "We are reinventing Man's relationship with the Earth," was their reply.

I was expecting to see emerge from the minibus the British Valkyrie who, having consumed my grappa straight from the bottle, said she had no time for Venice; I could see again her blue eyes seeped in mascara beneath her headband, her mahogany lips and, beneath a Carnaby Street frock so long that it mopped up the spittle on the ground, her large feet, cracked and filthy, and her silver-painted toes.

Their mouths full and belching forth garlic, the wandering Pithecanthropi, having accepted my invitation to lunch, recounted how they had cremated their companion in the ancient manner, on the shores of the Libyan Sea, as recently as Christmas, on a morning when, after consuming a great deal of mastic resin, ouzo, raki and heroin, she had not woken up. She was the daughter of an ecclesiastical peer, a life peer…. "That's actually what explains why she wanted to do away with herself…. Basically, she suffered from not being the daughter of a hereditary lord," said the driver of the minibus (Magdalen and BBC accent) as he scratched a head of hair that was as greasy as a poodle's; "People can say what they will, but *Burke's Peerage* was always her little red book…."

1971

TRIESTE, VILLA PERSEPHONE

THE VENICE-TRIESTE TRAIN puffs away for two hours as it follows the new motorway that links the two cities: Jesolo, Aquilea, Monfalcone. There are skyscrapers amid the cornfields, hidden canals in the vineyards, out of which rise up purple-tinged osiers and the stumps of willow trees. North of Venice industry extends indefinitely, stretching up the boot of the peninsula up to the top of the thigh, as far as Trieste.

I cross the city from which Stendhal, suspect and barely tolerated, fled as frequently as possible to Venice, on "unauthorised transfer" (this Foreign Office, Personnel Department style survives still), as soon as he had drawn his salary as consul *sans exequatur*; the Austrian police resented the bold Jacobin innovations of his *Histoire de la peinture*; this was the Stendhal who, in January 1831, was beginning a short story, *Les Mésaventures d'un Juif errant*, whose hero kept all he possessed in a violin case, and who, after each disaster that befell him, started again with nothing; a penniless Stendhal who was waiting for Louis-Philippe's government to pay him his wages so that he could buy shirts and who, like Joyce later on, was growing bored here; both men were biding their time awaiting the great regrading of human beings that is known as death. For Beyle, in Trieste, just as in Milan and Civitavecchia, it was always a case of an ill wind; it was one of fate's ironies that this eternal loser should have had ancestors whose name was Gagnon [*gagner* means to win]; what

The Grand Canal, Trieste

winnings could there be for someone who always took the wrong turnings in life. Beyle only ever loved Italy, which gave him the pox: "Kiss the lady," his mother told her little boy, aged five; instead, he bit the beautiful lady.

Through the villa's old Austrian postern gate, blinded by some tame turtledoves flying past, after crossing an old-fashioned park I reach the house belonging to my two female cousins by marriage that clings to a spur out of which some depressed looking trees, one on top of another, are searching for air, hemmed in as they are on all sides by twenty-storey blocks of flats that take advantage of the lack of foliage to peer out, between the bare branches, to see what is happening among their neighbours. It is the setting for a novel by Boylesve or Mathilde Serao. Quincunxes of rheumatic plane trees, their ancient scars filled with cement; the sea in the background; down below, the invisible city rumbles and weeps and murmurs, waiting for the moment to devour this old neighbourhood which makes its skyscrapers feel ashamed.

Intersected by two terraced ornamental ponds, and with box hedges shaped into balls, the path continues to climb up to the steps and towards the verandah of the Maria-Theresa dwelling, its pediment surmounted by some Vertumnus or other, eaten away by lichen, and flanked by fake Gothic towers from the time of the Emperor Franz-Josef, a noble residence from which the black smoke of its oil-fired heating system was now rising into the morning sun.

I come across my recluses, returning from their vegetable garden, carrying leeks in their baskets and holding between two fingers the first lady's slippers, which they have picked in their latest luxury, a greenhouse for orchids. At table in the vast dining-room, where the Viennese silverware, a relic of long-vanished banquets, Hélène's maternal grandmother—a grey tulle boa round her neck and with her hair cut short and very curly in the style of 1875 worn by the Tsarina Maria Feodorovna and her sister, Queen Alexandra of England,—gazes down on the ritual of the midday *dinner* (with soup), and *supper*, eaten at half past six in the evening.

Trieste is a strange pocket of civilisation indeed, a city that conceals itself, with a population that is silent, reticent and fearful, and which still has a flavour of bygone times, surviving as if she were an exception, her tail between her legs, embarrassed by her Latin character in the midst of the blond Slovenes, the new conquerors from the opposing shore.

My cousins link every general political matter to news from a member of their family, one that is dispersed widely from Canada to Bombay, or to those of it who were left behind after the anguish brought about by dictatorships of the left or the right.

"The Trautt…, you know: they were shot by the Nazis and thrown into a common grave…"

"Calliroe has just been thrown out of Alexandria, and given six hours' notice…"

"Aristides's memoirs have been banned in Athens…"

"Uncle André died in Vienna during the war, but what a wonderful way to go: he was listening to *Tristan* for the umpteenth time!"

"Dimitri is still doing hard labour on the Danube... When the Liberation came, he was able to identify his daughter because of a bracelet she wore on her arm."

On the menu for the day is chicken fried *à la triestine*, which reminds me slightly of the way they cook it in Virginia, and it is brought in ceremoniously by their old Dalmatian servant who, in 1944, opted to be Italian rather than become a Yugoslav. Seen from Trieste, Venice is the southernmost point of civilization.

"Martha Modl in *Parsifal*, now that was quite something!"

"Karajan is no longer the figure he was twenty years ago..."

"It's the soothing effect of that French woman..."

"What a mess she made of *The Valkyrie*!"

"Bertha's spending the summer at Irène's..."

"Sophie's in Rome..."

"Athénaïs is expecting her second, in Salzburg..."

"And Hilda's having hers in February, in Marseilles..."

My room is ready; a hot air heater that must be a hundred years old has emitted a column of black grime up the walls as far as the ceiling, where the Baroque period Venetian stucco is congested with Viennese Second Empire shells. There's a cup of herbal tea by my bedside light; my dear cousins had deliberated for a long time while they waited for me: "The last time he stayed, did he have camomile or *verveine*?" "No, I believe it was orange flower. I don't know what's happening to my memory!"

Tomorrow morning, we shall visit the Orthodox cemetery, as I had requested.

Greek independence, one hundred and fifty years ago, was responsible for a sudden dispersal of the Greek people; some set out once more on the ancient paths towards the Black Sea and the trade in wheat, from Galatz at the mouths of the Danube, as far as Odessa; others, feeling their way along the shores of the Mediterranean, like a blind man along a pavement, had gradually reached Trieste or Marseilles; later, they would venture as far as Bombay, London and New York. The E… had lived in Trieste, in their gardens on the headland, or in a house on Station Square that was as square and massive as a Genoese *palazzo*. Today, nothing is left apart from this villa, which is struggling to survive Italy's present plight. Perfect French is spoken here, as well as German with an Austrian accent, otherwise it is the Dalmatian spoken inTrieste. "In the spring of 1945," Triestinos say, "Field Marshal Alexander could have landed here, driven out the Croat partisans, and spared us forty days of deportations, pillaging and assassinations; in order to bar the way to Tito, who wanted the whole of Julian Veneto as far as Isonzo, thus presenting the West 'with a *fait accompli*', no less than three months of negotiations were required in Belgrade and in London. How feeble all these experts were, with their A zones and B zones! Trieste had to keep her head down in order to avoid being caught in the vast net which the Slavs wished to cast over her."

1971

A CEMETERY IN TRIESTE

WHAT FATE LIES in store for the souls belonging to these various cemeteries that separate the dead just as religions divide the living? Their tombs rise up along the slope of the hillside in a diversity that is the last luxury of the West: Italian, English, Russian necropolises, Jewish, Orthodox and Greek; all of them cared for, tended with flowers and set among wild grass, beneath ornamental holm oaks shaped like some dark drapery in the sunlight; the gardens of an archduke.

On this hill of the Dead, situated opposite Italy's last industrial valley, the cypress trees and cold marble slabs rise above the tall furnaces; here, stern mountains, balder than Mount Sinai, surround Trieste like an earthenware bowl that has been hardened by the sunlight and dried by the fearful northern bora. It's the same scenery that impressed Stendhal as he arrived from Venice: the lower slopes of the Carso, the white limestone amphitheatre, extend southwards along the Istrian coast. From Trieste, Stendhal wrote: "Here I confront barbarity."

I venture to fall in behind him.

The Italian-Yugoslav border divides two worlds; facing one is Asia, and those state-controlled lands that swallow up individuality as the plain imbibes the sand. Trieste is encircled, just as our little world is, just as Berlin is, and Israel, Madrid and the West; the rising tide does not attack head on, it takes the shore route, past millions of slip-knots, and progresses at a constant tangent; you might think that the ebb and flow of the Slavic sea, spurred on in turn by the Mongol ocean, bides its time; can no one see that it is advancing at the gallop?

With the city's unresolved status, and a truce lasting a quarter of a century that has not brought peace, Trieste is reminiscent of a forgotten corpse that has been left hanging at the top of the Adriatic ogive, in poignant dereliction, during an interminable diplomatic winter; through a blank wall, there are a few windows for foreigners, such as the sinister road that leads to Ljubljana, the tourists' entrance to the iron curtain. What does Tito want? Who shall succeed him? Supposing the Russians grow angry, what if the tanks of Prague ... Trieste wonders.

My own family is buried in France, more than a thousand kilometres from here, in boundless peace, beneath an almost wordless tombstone (this was what my father wanted), at Yerres, where my great-grandparents had acquired a small property, part of lands that had once belonged to the monastic order of the Camaldules,[1] which had been acquired by the State during the Revolution and later resold; because there was no more room in the family grave that I wished to be my final resting-place, I took refuge in the mausoleum of the E...family, offered to me by my cousins through marriage; it dates from the time of Franz-Josef, when Trieste was Austria's port on the Adriatic, when Trieste was still alive.

It is a noble stone pyramid, six metres high, a piece of typically Italian eloquence, above which an angel twice as tall as a human opens a black marble door to the after-life, as thick as that of an empty safe.

It is a tomb that is very different to the funereal sites of the great capital cities, with their crowded tombstones and their serried ranks of monuments that are frequented by enemies and strangers alike. The greenest of graveyards surrounded by the desert of the living. Blond or dark, Nordic or Latin, Orthodox or not, what will it matter beneath the ground?

That is where I shall lie, after this long accident that has been my life. My ashes, beneath this earth; an inscription in Greek will testify to the fact;[2] I shall be watched over by the Orthodox faith towards which Venice has conducted me, a religion whose joy lies in stillness and that continues to speak in the first language of the Gospels.

AFTERWORD

WHEN PAUL MORAND wrote *Venises*, at the age of eighty-two, he had finally achieved the recognition which had eluded him for a quarter of a century. His literary beginnings had been auspicious enough; many of his pre-war novels proved to be bestsellers. But after 1945, his reputation was ruined as the full extent of his wartime political activities came to light. Morand's unfailing support of the collaborationist regime of Pétain and Laval during the darkest hours of the Occupation, rewarded with an ambassadorship to Switzerland, and his subsequent denial of any wrongdoing, had resulted in a long self-imposed exile in Vevey, along the shores of Lac Léman. Morand's universe had collapsed. His books no longer sold, and he had to endure constant slights. Ironically, he was being persecuted for political beliefs which were never deeply held; rather, he had been opportunistic, short-sighted and foolish. Yet it is during those years of uncomfortable purgatory-like isolation that Morand wrote some of his best novels, and a masterpiece, *Hécate et ses Chiens*. His friends in France felt it was time to launch a campaign for his rehabilitation. After much discussion among literary and political circles, in 1968, General de Gaulle lifted his veto to Morand's election to the Académie Francaise. This bittersweet victory, far from taming him, gave the ageing writer a partial sense of vindication.

But perhaps there is another explanation for the lack of

esteem in which Morand was held until those late years. For much of his life Morand was preceded by his reputation: as a lightweight, a social figure who dabbled in literature—a certain kind of effortless but shallow travel-literature—the inveterate traveller, always hurried, restless, distracted, never grounded, never satisfied. Family connections, not to mention Marcel Proust's friendship with the young writer, were thought to have advanced his literary career, when he actually saw himself as a solitary, melancholy, introverted adolescent whose literary ascent was hesitant[1]. Indeed, in his *Journal inutile*, Morand recalls his distaste for the sort of social life which would become his trademark.

There is little doubt that Paul Morand lived a privileged childhood; summers were spent in Italy, and he was first taken to Venice at the age of sixteen (in September 1904). His parents rented a small apartment in a *palazzo* near the Traghetto San Maurizio and would return to it every year. Evenings were spent with Eugène Morand's artist-friends and poets, Brianchon, Dunoyer de Segonzac and the near-mythical figure of Henri de Régnier, among them. Together they formed a small circle of high-minded friends who shunned publicity and ostentation in favour of refined intellectual pleasures. Often they would congregate in the cafés of a deserted Piazza San Marco. Amidst the universal theatre of his adolescence loomed the eccentric, extravagant figure of Gabriele D'Annunzio,

---

[1] Paul Morand, *Journal inutile*, Gallimard Paris 2001, vol. I, 23rd May 1969, p.204

the poet of immense erudition and charm. It did not take long for the young Morand to fall under the spell of the city that worships beauty, and, being an avid reader, he delighted in Venice's historical associations with great literary figures, from Shakespeare, Goethe and Byron to Chateaubriand and Alfred de Musset. He also admired the more decadent figures of Casanova and Georges Sand. In Venice, the aspiring writer discovered the meanderings of a cultural tradition of which the *Laguna* itself provided a fascinating reflection in its layout. The sense of exhilaration derived from seeing the art of the great masters, from Crivelli to Tiepolo, from the innocence of the early masters to the decadence of the eighteenth century, helped define Morand's aestheticism. Crucial to him was the understanding that Art is the path towards self-realization. This notion never left him, even in the bleakest moments of his life. In Venice, he also met his first great love, the young painter Lisette Haas. The impression La Serenissima left on the adolescent was such that he would return to it throughout his life, not unlike a man who revisits an old flame. Venice appears to be the thread that binds together the disparate episodes of the novelist's long life.

At the end of 1910, Morand wrote his first novel, *Les Extravagants* (the manuscript, thought to have been destroyed in a fire, was found in Los Angeles in 1977 and published by Gallimard in 1986). In this first novel, Venice appears alongside London and Oxford as the city of youthful artistic and aesthetic dreams. But more interestingly, the same novel introduces Morand's "cosmopolitan" ideal, the meeting of culture and diplomacy among Europe's elite which he felt was rooted in the humanist tradition. The gradual disappearance of this fragile order is at the forefront of Morand's enquiry in *Venises*.

But this had not always been so. Let us not forget that Morand belongs to the generation that reached its maturity after 1918; after the abyss of the Great War, a sense of the absurdity of life had set in; this was the generation that longed to take flight from the horrors of the war and eventually lost itself through a frivolous lifestyle; the generation of Montparnasse and *Le Bœuf sur le Toit*, the age of Jazz. There is something deliberately lightweight and frivolous in Morand's novels of the Twenties, in their pursuit of speed and lightness. But in 1970 the situation was quite different. Written at the end of his life, *Venises* reveals much of Morand's precarious intellectual journey. For an author who was often accused of being superficial—although critics admired the polished, icy quality of his novels—the late work gains much in terms of depth and complexity, although never at the cost òf elegance. The author of *Tendres Stocks* has seen enough of the spectacle of life, and if metaphysical despair seems absent, fatigue has set in. It encompasses the singular—the unity of life—and the plural, the lack of coherence in life, which went hand in hand with a loss of faith in the Catholic Church. Perhaps it is not surprising that back in 1930, Morand found comfort in reading Nietzsche's *Will to Power* while sitting in a café on the Piazza San Marco. For Morand, the German philosopher's work put its faith in man's capacity to fight the demise of Western civilisation;

Self-portrait of Cecil Beaton at the Marco Polo Ball, Venice 1951

it called for the spiritual uprising of the old European nations. Morand found in Venice a greater sense of resilience than elsewhere; if people, treaties and wars come and go, la Serenissima had resisted the forces of Barbary. It was also one of Nietzsche's favourite cities, and the inspiration for a new, fascist Italy. Morand liked to quote him: "Men must be given back the courage of their natural instincts". In this context, Venice appears not only as the city of pleasure, but also as the city of Manin, Wagner, Nietzsche, D'Annunzio: Saint Mark against the East, the last fortification preserving the ancient European order. The Europe he knew could still be felt in Venice, though in 1951, at the Marco Polo Ball given by Charles de Besteigui, Morand was assailed by doubts. In the aftermath of a war that shattered much in his life, it became obvious to him that the aristocratic, cosmopolitan Europe that he admired had vanished. And there was no better vantage point than Venice to contemplate the ruins of an Empire.

The recent publication of Morand's *Journal inutile* gives us a sense of the difficult infancy of the manuscript. Although Morand had completed a draft in May 1970, he would revise the text well into the following year. It appears that he was careful not to offend the French war veterans; this concern seems to have been fuelled by the presence of numerous *Anciens Combattants* among his colleagues at the Académie Française. Morand also hesitated over the book's title: "My Venices. This title, so as to avoid *Venice and I*. An *s* on Venice? Such a beautiful word should not be interfered with; no *s*."[1] When *Venises*

[1] *Journal inutile*, 23rd May 1970, p.397

with an s finally came out in March 1971, to great acclaim, the first, rather modest printing of three thousand copies sold within days. The author wrote in his diary: "There's something of everything in *Venises*; frivolity, memories, meditations, serious themes, portraits, politics (without bias). It's a form that's hard to define. I believe its success is a result of this."[1]

Perhaps *Venises* is no more than a personal assemblage of various notations, quotes, descriptions, allusions, omissions. Many of Morand's remarks are likely to puzzle the mind of the modern reader but to the author this intellectual game is not gratuitous, for it refers to the values of the cultural elite of his youth. As such *Venises* has no equivalent in modern literature. And what remains firmly in the reader's mind is a rare sense of melancholy, elegance and poise. Morand liked to quote Chesterton: "Expensive clothes should always be worn casually."[2] What appealed to the readers of *Venises*—many of whom were too young to have known the upheaval created by two world wars— is a supreme combination of journalistic speed and sense of formula with the depth of a seventeenth century memorialist. For these readers, Morand's last book came as a relief to a generation more familiar with the left-wing, *engagé* literature of post-war France. No revolutionary dreams here—but a sense of beauty and elegance without equal in modern French literature. While in Venice, during the completion of this book, he wrote in his diary: "Yesterday evening, the sun was setting over St Mark's. I've

[1] *Journal inutile*, 30th March 1971, p.499
[2] *Journal inutile*, 26th April 1971, p.507

always loved that last ray of light on the domes, on the mosaics in the porch, on the patches of gold on the breasts of the green bronze horses in the quadriga ... Venice. The city I have loved above all others."[1]

OLIVIER BERGGRUEN

[1] *Journal inutile*, 14th July 1969, pp.234–5

NOTES

THE PALACE OF THE ANCIENTS

1. Writing prose without realising I was doing so, I discovered *implicit grammar*, the very latest thing today.

2. The École des Sciences Politiques.

3. Or again, *Mistrust when you don't know, suspect when you do.*

4. Herbert Marcuse (1898–1979) German-born, American writer and philosopher, influenced by both Marx and Freud; a fierce critic of affluent Western society, he became something of a hero to the youth culture of the 1960s. Morand, of course, was writing in 1970. [Tr.]

5. Now avenue Pierre-Ier-de-Serbie.

6. The office which supervises the finances of local authorities and monitors the use of public funds. [Tr.]

7. *Come, let us love, the nights are too fleeting, Come, let us dream, the days are too short...*[Tr.]

8. The École Centrale, the Paris *grande école* for highly qualified engineers. [Tr.]

9. In Stendhal's *The Charterhouse of Parma*. [Tr.]

10. The battle between the *vaporetti* and the gondoliers has been going on for sixty years, with the gondoliers' trade union trying to suggest that its rivals be diverted by the Giudecca.

11. The Fortune was re-gilded in 1971.

12. Nom de plume of the celebrated French anarchist François Koenigstein (1859–92), who was condemned to death and executed. [Tr.]

13. Émile Loubet (1838–1929) was elected as President of the Republic on the death of Félix Faure in 1899. It was he who reprieved Dreyfus. [Tr.]

14. Pierre Gouthière (1732–1813). One of the most famous ornamentalists of the late eighteenth century. He was the inventor of matt gilding. [Tr.]

15. Edmé Patrice Maurice MacMahon (1808–98) was descended from an Irish Jacobite family. He was appointed Marshal of France and Duke of Magenta after the Italian campaign of 1859, but was captured at Sedan in the Franco-German war of 1870-71. He later commanded the Versailles army that suppressed the Commune and was elected President of the Republic in 1873 for a period of seven years. [Tr.]

16. Or Il Parmigianino (1503–40), as he was known in Italy.

17. The École des Beaux-Arts is situated on the corner of the rue Bonaparte and the Quai Malaquais. [Tr.]

18. In 1970.

19. In 1970.

20. Unlike Paris, London has direct flights to Venice throughout the year.

21. Paul Cambon (1843–1924) was French Ambassador to London from 1898-1920 and helped bring about the Entente Cordiale of 1904. [Tr.]

22. Jean Eugène Robert-Houdin (1805–1871) achieved legendary fame as a conjuror and magician. [Tr.]

23. Antoine Rivarol (1753–1801) was a French writer famous for his conversational wit. He was the author of *Le Petit Almanach des grands hommes*, in which he directed his caustic sarcasm at Parisian society. [Tr.]

24. A punch distilled from cinnamon, cloves and various aromatic herbs, that was dyed red with kermes. [Tr.]

25. Except for Edmond Jaloux.

THE QUARANTINE FLAG

1. *Journal d'un attaché d'ambassade* (Gallimard).

2. See Guy Petrocini, *Les Mutineries de 1917*.

3. Georges Auric (1899–1983) was a composer. A friend of Darius

Milhaud and Erik Satie, he was one of the celebrated Groupe des Six. [Tr.]

4. Saint-John Perse.

5. Every salon at that time had its socialist: at Mme Straus's, it was Léon Blum; at Mme Ménard-Dorian's, Albert Thomas; at the Duchesse de Clermont-Tonnerre's, Rappoport; at Princesse Eugène Murat's, née Violette d'Elchingen, Bracke-Desrousseaux.

6. This was the title of Paul Morand's second collection of short stories (after *Tendres Stocks*, 1921), published in 1922. It was followed by another collection, *Fermé la nuit*, in 1924. Both were very successful. When Morand writes of the *Nuits*, he is presumably referring to both these books. [Tr.]

7. A reference to *Les Croix du bois*, Roland Dorgelès's novel about the First World War, which many believed should have been awarded the 1919 Prix Goncourt instead of Proust's *À l'ombre des jeunes filles en fleurs* [Tr.]

8. *October 1970.* Sheltering from an autumn storm in the Café de la Fenice, I perused the newspapers; I learned of the death of Dos Passos: "My ambition is to sing the Internationale", Dos Passos used to say, as a young man; he was then the equal of Hemingway, Scott Fitzgerald and Faulkner; Sartre considered him the best novelist of the time. From 1930 on Dos Passos opposed the "New Deal"; he considered the Second World War to be a catastrophe. "We can only regret that such an accomplished literary technician should have adopted such a narrow viewpoint and that the brilliant constellation of 1920 now shines so dimly ..." (*Herald Tribune*, 29 September 1970). "In 1929, Dos Passos unleashed a virulent critique of capitalist society; his work had a considerable impact. The Second World War was to bring about a true conversion in the writer.... At the same time as he altered his political views, Dos Passos seemed to lose his creative powers." (*Le Figaro*, 30 September 1970). Yesterday evening, on France-Inter, I listened to *Le Masque et la Plume*: "How can Ionesco still go on telling us about his death? He's been dead for ten years." I'm not very lucky with my friends who have advanced opinions.

9. The *grand corps de l'État* are senior civil servants recruited through the École Nationale d'Administration. [Tr.]

10. *pantouflage* is a term coined for those who leave the civil service to work in the private sector. [Tr.]

11. The Groupe des Six was a group of six young composers—Georges Auric, Louis Durey, Arthur Honegger, Darius Milhaud, François Poulenc and Germaine Tailleferre—that was centred around the figures of the composer Erik Satie and Jean Cocteau in the 1920s, and who became celebrated for their advanced ideas. [Tr.]

12. He kept open house, and at his table six blue angora cats would wander round among the plates.

13. Jacques Ange Gabriel (1698–1792). Celebrated French architect and interior designer. [Tr.]

14. At a banquet for three thousand guests, in the Grand Council chamber, the knives, forks, tablecloths and napkins were made from sugar, as were the epergnes and the statues of doges, planets and animals, modelled on drawings by Sansovino.

15. Morand was writing in 1970. Serge Lifar, Diaghilev's choreographer, died in Lausanne in 1986; Boris Kochno, a man closely associated with the ballet and the theatre throughout his life, died in Paris in 1990. [Tr.]

16. That of 1900.

17. See also what Proust has to say about Venice in Cahier 50 (explored so cleverly by Maurice Bardèche in his *Marcel Proust romancier*, vol. I, 1971).

18. Just one, at a crossroads at Rio Nuovo.

19. A Sevillan never travels up to Madrid; an inhabitant of Lausanne doesn't go to Geneva.

20. Daniele Manin (1804–57) Italian statesman who, after the Revolution of 1848, became the head of the Venetian Republic. He was active in the heroic Venetian resistance against Austria. [Tr.]

21. 1967. On the walls in Peking: "Kill the birds!"

22. 1970. The graffiti of the P.C. (il partito comunista) has returned: seen, yesterday, on a wall in the Brenta, the following invective, worthy of Alfieri: AMERICANI SERVI DELLA MORTE (Americans, lackeys of Death!).

MORTE IN MASCHERA

1. Jean-Etienne Liotard (1702–1789) was a Swiss artist and engraver widely admired for his precise and detailed portraits of Oriental people. [Tr.]

2. Which means broadly: "Whether I have the Palazzo Labia or not, I shall always be a Labia."[Tr.]

3. Marcel Jouhandeau (1888–1979) was a prolific French novelist and essayist who in certain of his books (in particular, *Chroniques maritales*, 1935) provided a ruthless analysis of the difficulties of conjugal life and his relationship with his wife Élise. [Tr.]

4. And if they adorn the summits of your palaces/It is by right of virtue, not by right of conquest. [Tr.]

5. "*Io sarò un Attila per lo stato veneto.*"

6. This was what I tried to explain to Paul Reynaud, as gently as possible, one spring evening in London in 1940, when he maintained that not a stone should be left standing in Paris. There had been four of us dining at Ava Wigram's house, with Hore-Belisha; the British Secretary of State for War had arrived late after making a speech in the House of Commons and had immediately wanted to hear himself again, insisting that a wireless set be placed on the table, thereby making all conversation impossible. Hore-Belisha approved of Reynaud. Both men are dead; Paris remains.

IT'S EASIER TO START THAN IT IS TO END

1. A religious order of monks and hermits, founded by St Romuald in 1010, in the valley of Camaldoli in Tuscany. [Tr.]

2. In translation this reads: Traveller go on your way with her, who was, who is, who will for ever be your guardian angel. [Tr.]

HENRY JAMES

Letters from the Palazzo Barbaro

HENRY JAMES first came to Venice as a tourist
but was soon fascinated by the city and particularly by the splendid gothic Palazzo Barbaro,
situated on the Grand Canal, home of the expa-
triate American Curtis family. In the gilded and
stucco salon of the palace, Sargent painted family portraits and Browning read his poems. James
frequently returned to the palace to write, com-
pleting *The Aspern Papers* there. This selection of
letters covers the period 1869–1907.

The letters have been selected and edited
by Rosella Mamoli Zorzi, Professor of Anglo-
American Literature at the University of Venice,
Ca' Foscari. The late Leon Edel, the great James
biographer and editor, provided an Introduction
to this volume which contains previously unpublished manuscript letters. Patricia Curtis, a member of the present generation of the family living
in the palace, has contributed an Afterword spe-
cially written for the Pushkin Press edition.

ISBN 1-901285-07-3 · 224pp · £10/$14